THE SPARK WITHIN

NURTURING CREATIVITY IN CHILDREN

DR. MINAKSHI BANSAL

DEDICATION

To my children, whose boundless curiosity and creativity inspire me every day. You are the spark that lights up my world.

To my parents, who nurtured my love for learning and always encouraged me to explore my passions.

To all the dedicated educators and caregivers who tirelessly support and nurture the potential within every child. Your unwavering commitment and love make all the difference.

And to every child out there, may you always have the freedom to dream, the courage to create, and the support to turn your visions into reality.

♡♡♡

Contents

Prayer   *vii*

About The Author   *ix*

Preface   *xiii*

1. The Importance Of Creativity In Childhood   1

Part 1

2. Creating A Creative Environment At Home   9

Part 2

3. Encouraging Imaginative Play   17

Part 3

4. Art And Craft Activities   25

Part 4

5. Music And Movement   33

Part 5

6. Storytelling And Creative Writing   41

Part 6

7. Nature And Outdoor Exploration   49

Part 7

8. Building And Construction Play   57

Part 8

9. Creative Problem-Solving Skills   65

Part 9

10. Role-Playing And Drama   73

Part 10

11. Fostering A Growth Mindset   81

Part 11

12. Technology And Digital Creativity   89

Contents

Part 12

  13. Collaboration And Teamwork   97

Part 13

  14. Creative Cooking And Baking   105

Part 14

  15. Exploring Different Cultures   113

Part 15

  16. Balancing Structure And Freedom   123

Part 16

  17. Supporting Individual Interests   131

Part 17

  18. The Power Of Questions   139

Part 18

  19. Creative Challenges And Competitions   147

Part 19

  20. Celebrating Creative Achievements   155

Part 20

  21. SUMMARY   163

Citation and References   169

Other Books of the Author   171

CONTACT   177

Prayer

"Om Bhadram Karnebhih Shrinuyama Devah

Bhadram Pashyemakshabhiryajatrah

Sthirairangais Tushtuvamsastanubhih

Vyashema Devahitam Yadayuh

Svasti Na Indro Vriddhashravah

Svasti Nah Pusha Vishwavedah

Svasti Nastarkshyo Arishtanemih

Svasti No Brihaspatir Dadhatu

Om Shantih Shantih Shantih"

This mantra is a prayer for universal well-being, invoking the blessings of various deities for protection, health, and happiness. It emphasizes the importance of experiencing the auspicious through all senses and living a life aligned with divine purpose. The repetition of "Shantih" at the end signifies a deep desire for peace in the individual, the environment, and the universe at large. This mantra is often recited as a prayer for peace, prosperity, and the physical and spiritual well-being of all beings.

ᐅᐅᐅ

About The Author

This book represents the culmination of extensive research and meticulous analysis, incorporating a diverse range of sources, including numerous books, scholarly studies, and personal experiences. Additionally, I have scoured various websites to gather relevant information and data essential for the compilation of this work. I have taken every precaution to ensure the accuracy of the information presented and have diligently cited all sources to acknowledge their contributions.

From her earliest days, Minakshi was distinguished by an insatiable appetite for reading. Her literary universe was inhabited by characters and narratives that spanned ethical tales, motivational and inspirational stories, and the mythic parables imbued with life lessons. This voracious reading habit was not merely for personal edification but was driven by a desire to distill and disseminate the essence of these narratives to foster the development of students and peers alike. She was particularly captivated by the lives and teachings of historical figures and spiritual leaders such as Adi Shankaracharya, Swami Vivekananda, Dr. APJ Abdul Kalam, Mahamana Pandit Madan Mohan Malviya, Mahatma Gandhi, Sardar Vallabhai Patel, and Vinoba Bhave, among others. Their philosophies and life stories fueled her ambition to embody their ideals of resilience, selflessness, and relentless pursuit of knowledge.

Dr. Minakshi's academic and practical engagement with psychology has been equally noteworthy. As a research scholar, her focus has been on exploring the intricate tapestry of the human psyche, aiming to unlock the potential for psychological well-being and societal harmony. Her scholarly work is complemented by her active involvement in social work, where she employs her academic insights to make tangible differences in the lives of the underprivileged. Her endeavours in social work are characterized by an innovative approach that combines traditional wisdom with contemporary psychological practices to address the multifaceted challenges faced by these communities.

Her artistic talents, another facet of her diverse capabilities, are not merely a personal passion but also serve as a medium through which she communicates and connects with others. Her art, rich in symbolism and emotional depth, reflects her philosophical inquiries and social concerns, offering viewers a glimpse into the breadth of her intellect and the depth of her compassion.

In addition to her contributions to the arts and social sciences, Dr. Minakshi has embraced the healing arts of Pranic Healing, mastering the techniques developed by Master Choa Kok Sui. This practice, which focuses on the manipulation of Prana or life energy to heal the body and aura, has been both a personal journey of discovery and a means through which she extends her healing touch to others. Her proficiency in Pranic Healing is complemented by her advocacy and teaching of various forms of meditation aimed at rejuvenation, personal betterment, and the cultivation of harmony within individuals and communities alike.

Dr. Minakshi's life is a narrative of relentless pursuit, not just of personal achievement but of the upliftment and empowerment of society at large. Her diverse interests and talents—spanning the arts, literature, psychology, and the healing practices—converge on a singular path of service. She embodies the spirit of the luminaries who inspired her, channelling their legacy through her actions and teachings. Through her books, art, and social initiatives, she continues to inspire a new generation to embark on their own journeys of self-discovery, resilience, and altruism.

Her commitment to social betterment, particularly her focus on uplifting underprivileged children, reflects a deep understanding of the transformative potential of education and personal development. By integrating her knowledge of psychology, her artistic sensibilities, and her healing practices, Dr. Bansal has developed a holistic approach to social work that addresses both the immediate needs and the long-term well-being of the communities she serves.

As an author, Dr. Minakshi's writings offer a blend of inspirational insights, practical wisdom, and reflective contemplations drawn from her extensive reading and life experiences. Her books serve as a guide for those seeking to navigate the complexities of life with grace, resilience, and purpose. Through her narratives, she extends an invitation to her readers to explore the depths of their own potential and to contribute meaningfully to the collective well-being of society.

In Dr. Minakshi Bansal, we find a remarkable synthesis of the artist, the scholar, the healer, and the social activist. Her life's work stands as a beacon of hope and a source of inspiration for individuals seeking to make a difference in the world. Her story is a compelling reminder of the power of individual action, rooted in compassion and driven by a profound commitment to the betterment of humanity. Dr. Minakshi's legacy is not just in the tangible outcomes of her efforts but in the enduring spirit of inquiry, empathy, and service that she embodies.

ᐯᐯᐯ

Preface

The journey of writing this book has been both a deeply personal and profoundly enlightening experience. As an educator and a mother, I have long been captivated by the boundless potential that resides within every child. Watching my own children explore the world with wide-eyed wonder and uninhibited curiosity, I have often found myself marveling at their innate creativity and the sheer joy they derive from discovering new things. This book is a culmination of my observations, experiences, and research, all aimed at understanding how best to nurture the spark of creativity that exists within every child.

Creativity is not just a skill; it is a way of thinking, a way of approaching the world. It is the ability to see beyond the obvious, to connect seemingly unrelated ideas, and to imagine possibilities that do not yet exist. It is the driving force behind innovation, problem-solving, and personal expression. In a rapidly changing world where adaptability and innovation are more important than ever, fostering creativity in our children is not just beneficial—it is essential.

Throughout my career, I have had the privilege of working with many children, each with their unique blend of talents, interests, and quirks. This diversity has reinforced my belief that creativity is not confined to the arts but is a universal trait that can manifest in countless ways. Whether it is a child meticulously building a complex structure out of blocks, composing a heartfelt piece of music, solving a tricky math problem, or inventing a new game with friends, creativity is at play. This book seeks to celebrate and cultivate that creativity, providing practical insights and strategies for parents, educators, and anyone else who plays a role in a child's development.

One of the central themes that emerged during my research is the importance of balancing structure and freedom. Children need routines and boundaries to feel secure and understand expectations, but they also need the freedom to explore, experiment, and make mistakes. This balance is crucial for fostering an environment where creativity can thrive. Too much structure can stifle creativity, while too much freedom without guidance can lead to frustration and confusion. Finding the right balance requires patience, observation, and a willingness to adapt as children grow and their needs evolve.

Another key insight is the power of questions. Encouraging children to ask questions and explore their curiosity is one of the most effective ways to stimulate creative thinking. Questions are the starting point for inquiry and discovery, driving children to seek out new information, challenge assumptions, and develop their understanding of the world. As adults, our role is to foster this curiosity by providing answers when we can, guiding children to find their own answers when appropriate, and most importantly, by modeling a curious and questioning mindset ourselves.

Supporting individual interests is also critical. Every child has unique passions and talents, and it is our responsibility to nurture these interests and provide opportunities for children to explore and develop them. This means paying attention to what excites and engages each child, offering resources and encouragement, and celebrating their efforts and achievements. It also means being flexible and open-minded, recognizing that a child's interests may change over time and being willing to adapt our support accordingly.

Creative challenges and competitions can be powerful tools for development, providing opportunities for children to push their boundaries, develop new skills, and gain confidence in their abilities. These experiences teach children the value of effort and perseverance, the importance of learning from mistakes, and the joy of achieving a hard-earned goal. However, it is important to approach these activities with a focus on growth and learning rather than winning, ensuring that all children feel valued and supported regardless of the outcome.

Exploring different cultures is another enriching experience that can significantly enhance a child's creativity. Exposure to diverse perspectives, traditions, and ways of thinking broadens a child's understanding of the world and sparks new ideas and connections. It fosters empathy, open-mindedness, and a deeper appreciation for the richness of human experience. Encouraging children to learn about and engage with different cultures through travel, literature, art, music, and personal interactions can have a profound impact on their creative development.

Nature and outdoor exploration offer countless opportunities for creative play and discovery. The natural world is a vast, ever-changing playground that stimulates the senses and inspires the imagination. Whether it is building a fort in the woods, observing wildlife, or simply enjoying the beauty of a sunset, time spent in nature fosters a sense of wonder and curiosity. It also provides a much-needed balance to the increasingly digital and structured environments that many children experience.

Storytelling and creative writing are powerful ways for children to express themselves, explore their thoughts and emotions, and develop their language skills. These activities encourage children to use their imagination, create characters and worlds, and convey their ideas in compelling ways. They also provide a safe space for children to process their experiences and share their perspectives. Supporting children in their storytelling and writing efforts, whether through encouragement, feedback, or providing opportunities for them to share their work, can have a lasting impact on their creative and emotional development.

Music and movement activities are essential for fostering creativity and physical development. Engaging with music through singing, playing instruments, and dancing helps children develop their auditory and motor skills, while also providing a powerful outlet for emotional expression. These activities promote coordination, rhythm, and a sense of joy and connection. Encouraging children to explore different types of music and movement, and providing opportunities for them to create and perform, helps them develop a deep appreciation for the arts and their own creative potential.

Art and craft activities offer endless possibilities for creative exploration. Working with different materials and techniques allows children to experiment, take risks, and develop their artistic skills. These activities also provide opportunities for problem-solving and critical thinking, as children figure out how to bring their ideas to life. By providing a variety of materials and encouraging children to follow their interests and instincts, we can help them develop their creativity and confidence.

Imaginative play and role-playing are fundamental to children's social and emotional development. These activities allow children to explore different roles, scenarios, and perspectives, helping them develop empathy, communication skills, and a deeper understanding of the world around them. They also provide a safe space for children to express their emotions and work through challenges. Supporting imaginative play by providing props, creating a conducive environment, and participating in the play when appropriate, helps children fully engage in these creative activities.

Building and construction play is another important aspect of creative development. These activities help children develop spatial awareness, fine and gross motor skills, and problem-solving abilities. They also encourage creativity and innovation, as children design and build their own structures. Providing a variety of materials and opportunities for building and construction play, and encouraging children to experiment and take risks, helps them develop their skills and confidence.

Supporting a growth mindset is crucial for fostering creativity and resilience. Children who believe that their abilities can be developed through effort and learning are more likely to take on challenges, persist in the face of setbacks, and see failure as a valuable part of the learning process. Encouraging a growth mindset involves praising effort and progress rather than innate talent, modeling a positive attitude towards challenges, and providing opportunities for children to learn and grow.

Technology and digital creativity offer exciting opportunities for children to explore new forms of expression and innovation. Digital tools and platforms can enhance children's creative skills, provide new ways to collaborate and share their work, and open up new possibilities for learning and exploration. However, it is important to balance digital activities with hands-on, real-world experiences, and to guide children in using technology responsibly and creatively.

Collaboration and teamwork are essential skills for creative development. Working with others on creative projects teaches children the value of different perspectives, the importance of communication and cooperation, and the joy of shared achievement. Providing opportunities for collaborative activities, such as group projects, performances, and community events, helps children develop these skills and build strong, supportive relationships.

Celebrating creative achievements is crucial for reinforcing the value of creativity and encouraging further exploration. Recognizing and honoring children's creative efforts, whether through praise, awards, exhibitions, or performances, boosts their self-esteem and motivates them to continue pursuing their interests. These celebrations also provide opportunities for children to share their work with others, receive positive feedback, and feel valued for their contributions.

In writing this book, I have drawn on my experiences as an educator, a mother, and a lifelong learner. I have been inspired by the incredible creativity and resilience of the children I have had the privilege to work with and by the dedication and support of parents and educators who are committed to nurturing the spark within each child. My hope is that this book will provide valuable insights, practical strategies, and inspiration for those who seek to foster creativity in children and help them reach their full potential.

As we embark on this journey together, let us remember that every child has a unique spark of creativity waiting to be nurtured. By providing a supportive and stimulating environment, encouraging exploration and expression, and celebrating each child's unique contributions, we can help them develop the skills, confidence, and resilience they need to thrive in an ever-changing world. It is my sincere hope that this book will serve as a guide and a source of inspiration for parents, educators, and anyone who plays a role in a child's development. Together, let us nurture the spark within every child and help them shine.

Dr. Minakshi Bansal
Social Activist
Ahmedabad, Gujarat, Bharat

ONE

The Importance of Creativity in Childhood

Creativity is an essential component of a child's development, playing a crucial role in shaping their cognitive, emotional, and social growth. The importance of creativity in childhood cannot be overstated, as it lays the foundation for critical thinking, problem-solving, and adaptability—skills that are indispensable in today's rapidly changing world. Creativity allows children to express themselves, understand their environment, and engage with others in meaningful ways. By fostering creativity, we help children develop a sense of identity, confidence, and a love for learning that will serve them throughout their lives.

Creativity in children is not just about producing art or engaging in imaginative play; it encompasses a broad spectrum of activities and ways of thinking that enable children to explore new ideas, solve problems in innovative ways, and make connections between seemingly unrelated concepts. This kind of thinking is crucial for cognitive development. When children engage in creative activities, they use multiple areas of their brain, enhancing neural connections and promoting cognitive flexibility. This mental agility is vital for learning and adapting to new situations, helping children to think outside the box and approach challenges with an open mind.

One of the most significant benefits of nurturing creativity in children is its impact on problem-solving skills. Creative thinking involves looking at problems from different angles, generating multiple solutions, and evaluating the potential outcomes of each option. This process helps children develop resilience and perseverance, as they learn that failure is not a setback but an opportunity to try again with a different approach. By encouraging creative problem-solving, we equip children with the tools they need to navigate the complexities of life, both in their personal and academic pursuits.

Creativity also plays a pivotal role in emotional development. Through creative expression, children learn to process and articulate their feelings, which is essential for emotional regulation and mental health. Whether through drawing, writing, music, or drama, creative activities provide an outlet for children to explore their emotions in a safe and constructive manner. This self-expression helps them understand and cope with their feelings, reducing anxiety and building emotional resilience. Additionally, creativity fosters empathy by allowing children to put themselves in others' shoes, enhancing their ability to understand and relate to different perspectives.

Socially, creativity helps children develop important interpersonal skills. Collaborative creative activities, such as group art projects, drama, or music ensembles, teach children how to communicate effectively, share ideas, and work together towards a common goal. These experiences build teamwork and cooperation, essential skills for building healthy relationships and functioning in group settings. Moreover, creative activities often involve negotiation and compromise, helping children learn to navigate social dynamics and develop a sense of fairness and empathy.

Creativity also promotes self-esteem and confidence. When children engage in creative endeavors and see their ideas come to life, they gain a sense of accomplishment and pride. This positive reinforcement encourages them to take risks and try new things, fostering a growth mindset. A growth mindset, the belief that abilities and intelligence can be developed through effort and perseverance, is crucial for lifelong learning and success. By celebrating creative achievements, we help children build a strong sense of self-worth and the confidence to pursue their passions.

Furthermore, creativity enriches the learning experience by making it more engaging and enjoyable. Traditional educational methods often focus on rote memorization and standardized testing, which can be stifling for many children. Incorporating creative activities into the curriculum can make learning more dynamic and interactive, sparking curiosity and a love for knowledge. When children are actively involved in their learning process, they are more likely to retain information and develop a deeper understanding of the subject matter. Creative teaching methods, such as project-based learning, storytelling, and hands-on experiments, can transform the classroom into a vibrant and stimulating environment that fosters intellectual growth.

In addition to its cognitive, emotional, and social benefits, creativity is also essential for cultural and personal identity. Creative activities allow children to explore and celebrate their cultural heritage, traditions, and values. Through art, music, dance, and storytelling, children can connect with their roots and develop a sense of pride in their cultural identity. This cultural awareness fosters inclusivity and appreciation for diversity, helping children to become more open-minded and respectful of different backgrounds and viewpoints.

Moreover, creativity helps children discover their passions and interests. By providing opportunities for creative exploration, we allow children to experiment with different activities and find what truly excites and inspires them. This self-discovery is crucial for personal growth and development, as it helps children build a sense of purpose and direction. Pursuing their creative interests can lead to the development of specialized skills and talents, which can be further nurtured and refined as they grow.

In today's digital age, the importance of creativity is even more pronounced. Technology has transformed the way we live, work, and learn, and creative thinking is essential for navigating this ever-evolving landscape. Digital tools and platforms offer new avenues for creative expression and collaboration, enabling children to explore innovative ways of thinking and problem-solving. By integrating technology with creative activities, we can prepare children for the challenges and opportunities of the future, equipping them with the skills they need to thrive in a digital world.

Despite its many benefits, creativity is often undervalued in traditional education systems. The emphasis on standardized testing and academic performance can stifle creativity, as children are pressured to conform to rigid expectations and benchmarks. To truly nurture creativity, we must adopt a more holistic approach to education that values and encourages creative thinking. This involves creating a supportive and stimulating environment that allows children the freedom to explore, experiment, and take risks without fear of failure or judgment.

Parents, educators, and caregivers play a crucial role in fostering creativity in children. By providing opportunities for creative exploration and supporting their creative endeavors, we can help children develop the skills and confidence they need to become innovative and adaptable individuals. Encouraging creativity requires patience, understanding, and a willingness to embrace the messiness and unpredictability that often accompanies the creative process. It also involves recognizing and celebrating the unique strengths and talents of each child, allowing them to shine in their own way.

In conclusion, the importance of creativity in childhood cannot be overstated. Creativity is fundamental to cognitive, emotional, and social development, providing children with the tools they need to navigate the complexities of life. By fostering creativity, we help children develop critical thinking, problem-solving, and adaptability, essential skills for success in today's rapidly changing world. Creativity also promotes emotional resilience, empathy, and social skills, contributing to overall well-being and healthy relationships. Furthermore, creativity enriches the learning experience, making it more engaging and enjoyable, and helps children discover their passions and cultural identity.

In the digital age, creative thinking is more important than ever, enabling children to thrive in an ever-evolving landscape. To truly nurture creativity, we must adopt a holistic approach to education that values and encourages creative thinking, creating a supportive and stimulating environment for children to explore and grow. By doing so, we can help children unlock their full potential and become innovative and adaptable individuals, ready to face the challenges and opportunities of the future.

ᗮᗮᗮ

"Creativity is the spark that lights up a child's world. It fuels their curiosity and drives them to explore the unknown. Nurturing this spark is the key to unlocking their boundless potential."

❥❥❥

TWO

CREATING A CREATIVE ENVIRONMENT AT HOME

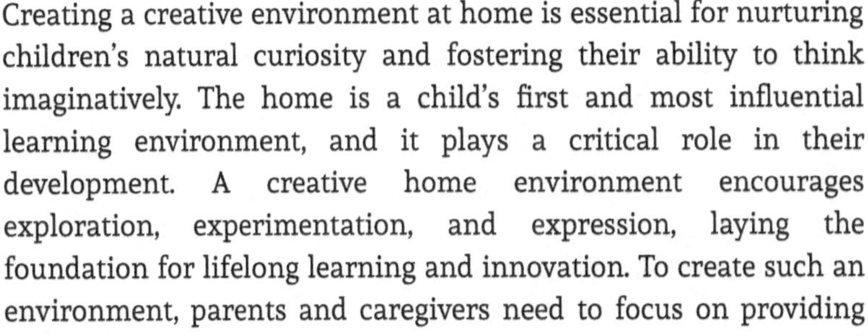

Creating a creative environment at home is essential for nurturing children's natural curiosity and fostering their ability to think imaginatively. The home is a child's first and most influential learning environment, and it plays a critical role in their development. A creative home environment encourages exploration, experimentation, and expression, laying the foundation for lifelong learning and innovation. To create such an environment, parents and caregivers need to focus on providing the right physical space, fostering a supportive atmosphere, and offering diverse and stimulating experiences.

One of the fundamental aspects of creating a creative environment at home is the physical space. A dedicated area for creative activities can make a significant difference. This space doesn't need to be large or elaborate; it can be a corner of a room or a specific table designated for creative projects. The key is to make it inviting and accessible. Having a variety of art supplies, such as crayons, markers, paints, paper, glue, and scissors, readily available encourages children to engage in creative activities spontaneously. Organizing these supplies in a way that is easy for children to access and tidy up promotes independence and a sense of ownership over their creative process.

In addition to art supplies, incorporating other materials that stimulate creativity is beneficial. Items like building blocks, LEGO sets, puzzles, and craft kits provide opportunities for hands-on exploration and construction. These materials help develop fine motor skills and spatial awareness while also encouraging problem-solving and innovative thinking. Rotating these materials periodically can keep the creative space fresh and exciting, preventing children from becoming bored with the same items.

Beyond the physical setup, the atmosphere in the home plays a crucial role in fostering creativity. Children thrive in environments where they feel safe, supported, and free to express themselves without fear of judgment or failure. Encouraging a positive and open-minded attitude towards creativity is essential. Parents and caregivers can model this behavior by expressing their own creativity and showing appreciation for diverse forms of creative expression. When children see adults valuing and engaging in creative activities, they are more likely to feel inspired and confident in exploring their own creativity.

Providing positive reinforcement and celebrating children's creative efforts is another important aspect of fostering a supportive atmosphere. Instead of focusing solely on the final product, it's important to recognize and praise the effort, process, and thought behind their creations. This approach helps build children's confidence and encourages them to take risks and experiment with new ideas. Displaying their artwork and creations in the home can also give children a sense of pride and accomplishment, reinforcing the value of their creative efforts.

Creating a creative environment at home also involves offering diverse and stimulating experiences that inspire imagination and curiosity. Exposure to different forms of art, music, literature, and cultural experiences can broaden children's horizons and spark new ideas. Visiting museums, attending performances, reading books, and exploring nature are all activities that can provide rich and varied sources of inspiration. These experiences can be discussed and reflected upon at home, encouraging children to think critically and make connections between what they have seen and their own creative projects.

Incorporating creativity into everyday activities is another effective way to nurture a creative environment. Cooking, for example, can be a highly creative activity that involves experimenting with different ingredients, flavors, and presentation styles. Involving children in the kitchen and encouraging them to come up with their own recipes or ways to decorate dishes can make cooking a fun and imaginative experience. Gardening is another activity that can stimulate creativity, as children can design their own garden layouts, choose plants, and learn about the growth process. These everyday activities provide practical opportunities for creative thinking and problem-solving.

Encouraging imaginative play is also crucial for fostering creativity at home. Children naturally engage in imaginative play, which allows them to explore different scenarios, roles, and perspectives. Providing them with costumes, props, and open-ended toys can enhance their imaginative play experiences. Simple items like cardboard boxes, fabric scraps, and household objects can be transformed into anything from pirate ships to magical castles in the hands of imaginative children. Allowing children the freedom to direct their own play and come up with their own stories and scenarios promotes creative thinking and self-expression.

Limiting screen time and encouraging hands-on, interactive activities is another important consideration. While technology can offer valuable creative tools, it's important to strike a balance and ensure that children have ample opportunities for physical and imaginative play. Encouraging outdoor activities and unstructured playtime can help children develop a sense of wonder and curiosity about the world around them. Nature provides endless opportunities for creative exploration, from collecting and arranging natural materials to observing wildlife and creating outdoor art installations.

In addition to providing diverse experiences and materials, it's important to support children's creative pursuits by being actively involved and engaged. Taking the time to participate in creative activities with children can strengthen the parent-child bond and provide valuable guidance and encouragement. Asking open-ended questions about their projects, offering constructive feedback, and showing genuine interest in their creative ideas can make a significant difference in their creative development. By being involved, parents and caregivers can help children overcome challenges, refine their skills, and build confidence in their creative abilities.

Another key aspect of creating a creative environment at home is fostering a growth mindset. Encouraging children to view mistakes and failures as opportunities for learning and growth rather than setbacks is essential for developing resilience and perseverance. When children understand that creativity involves experimentation and that not every attempt will be successful, they are more likely to take risks and try new things. Emphasizing the value of the creative process over the final product helps children develop a love for learning and a willingness to explore their ideas without fear of failure.

Finally, it's important to recognize and support each child's unique creative interests and talents. Every child is different, and what inspires one may not resonate with another. Paying attention to children's individual preferences and providing opportunities for them to explore their interests can help them develop a deeper connection to their creative pursuits. Whether a child is passionate about drawing, music, building, or storytelling, offering tailored support and resources can help them flourish and reach their full creative potential.

Creating a creative environment at home involves a combination of providing the right physical space, fostering a supportive atmosphere, and offering diverse and stimulating experiences. By making creative materials accessible, encouraging a positive attitude towards creativity, and incorporating creativity into everyday activities, parents and caregivers can nurture children's natural curiosity and imagination. Supporting imaginative play, limiting screen time, and being actively involved in children's creative pursuits further enhance their development.

Fostering a growth mindset and recognizing each child's unique interests and talents are also crucial for helping them reach their full creative potential. By creating a home environment that values and encourages creativity, we can help children develop the skills, confidence, and passion they need to thrive in all areas of life.

"Children thrive when they have the freedom to explore and the structure to feel secure. Balancing these elements fosters resilience and creativity. It is in this balance that they find their true potential."

❦❦❦

THREE

ENCOURAGING IMAGINATIVE PLAY

Encouraging imaginative play is essential for the holistic development of children, as it fosters creativity, cognitive growth, emotional regulation, and social skills. Imaginative play, also known as pretend play or make-believe play, involves children using their imagination to create scenarios, roles, and narratives, often using toys, props, or even nothing at all. This type of play is not just about entertainment; it serves as a critical foundation for learning and development.

One of the key benefits of imaginative play is the enhancement of creativity. When children engage in make-believe scenarios, they are free to invent worlds, characters, and stories. This freedom to create without boundaries allows children to explore different ideas, experiment with various outcomes, and develop their creative thinking skills. Unlike structured activities, imaginative play does not have predetermined rules or objectives, giving children the liberty to follow their interests and impulses. This unstructured environment encourages children to think divergently, generating multiple solutions to problems and exploring a wide range of possibilities.

Imaginative play also plays a crucial role in cognitive development. During pretend play, children often imitate adult behaviors and scenarios, which helps them understand the world around them. For instance, playing house allows children to explore family roles, routines, and relationships, helping them make sense of their own experiences. This type of play supports the development of symbolic thinking, where children learn to use one object to represent another. For example, a stick can become a sword, a doll can become a baby, and a blanket can become a superhero cape. This ability to think symbolically is fundamental for later academic skills, such as reading, writing, and math, as it involves understanding and manipulating abstract concepts.

Another cognitive benefit of imaginative play is the development of language and communication skills. When children engage in pretend play, they often create dialogues, narrate stories, and negotiate roles with their playmates. This verbal interaction enhances their vocabulary, sentence structure, and conversational skills. Additionally, taking on different roles and perspectives during play helps children develop empathy and theory of mind—the ability to understand that others have thoughts, feelings, and perspectives different from their own. These skills are critical for effective communication and social interactions.

Emotionally, imaginative play provides children with a safe space to explore and express their feelings. Through role-playing, children can act out scenarios that may be confusing, scary, or overwhelming in real life. For example, a child who is anxious about a doctor's visit might play doctor with their toys, giving them a sense of control and helping them process their fears. By externalizing their emotions through play, children can better understand and manage their feelings. This process of emotional exploration and expression is essential for developing emotional regulation and resilience.

Imaginative play also fosters social skills and cooperation. When children engage in group pretend play, they learn to share, take turns, negotiate roles, and collaborate on creating and sustaining play scenarios. These interactions require children to communicate effectively, resolve conflicts, and understand the perspectives of their playmates. Through these social interactions, children develop important social competencies, such as empathy, cooperation, and problem-solving skills. These skills are crucial for building and maintaining healthy relationships throughout their lives.

Parents and caregivers play a vital role in encouraging imaginative play. One of the most effective ways to promote this type of play is by providing a variety of open-ended toys and materials that can be used in multiple ways. Items such as building blocks, dolls, action figures, dress-up clothes, art supplies, and household objects can all inspire imaginative scenarios. Open-ended toys do not have a specific purpose or set of instructions, allowing children to use them creatively and according to their imagination.

In addition to providing materials, creating a conducive environment for imaginative play is important. This involves setting aside time and space where children can engage in uninterrupted play. A dedicated play area with accessible toys and materials can encourage children to initiate and sustain their imaginative activities. It's also beneficial to limit screen time and structured activities, giving children the freedom and opportunity to engage in self-directed play.

Parents and caregivers can also actively participate in imaginative play to support and extend children's creativity. By joining in the play, adults can model imaginative thinking, introduce new ideas, and provide gentle guidance. For instance, if a child is playing store, a parent might take on the role of a customer, asking questions and making purchases to enrich the play scenario. This involvement not only enhances the play experience but also strengthens the parent-child bond.

It's important, however, to strike a balance between guiding the play and allowing children to lead. While adult participation can enrich the play, children should be given the autonomy to direct the scenarios and make decisions. This autonomy is crucial for developing their confidence and sense of agency. Parents and caregivers should follow the child's lead, offering support and suggestions when needed but avoiding taking over the play.

Encouraging imaginative play also involves being attentive and responsive to children's interests and cues. By observing what captures their attention and sparks their imagination, parents and caregivers can provide materials and opportunities that align with these interests. For example, if a child shows an interest in dinosaurs, providing dinosaur figurines, books, and props can inspire imaginative scenarios and deepen their engagement.

Incorporating elements of storytelling into play can further enhance children's imaginative experiences. Storytelling allows children to create narratives, develop characters, and explore different themes. Parents and caregivers can encourage storytelling by asking open-ended questions, prompting children to elaborate on their play scenarios, and creating storybooks together. This process of creating and sharing stories not only fosters creativity but also supports language development and narrative skills.

Outdoor play offers another rich avenue for imaginative exploration. Nature provides endless opportunities for children to engage their senses and imagination. A simple trip to the park or a walk in the woods can inspire imaginative play, whether it's pretending to be explorers, building fairy houses, or creating nature art. The natural environment stimulates curiosity and creativity, providing a dynamic and ever-changing backdrop for children's imaginative adventures.

It's also beneficial to introduce children to various forms of creative expression, such as art, music, dance, and drama. These activities allow children to explore different ways of expressing their ideas and emotions, enriching their imaginative play. For example, listening to music can inspire children to create dance routines or put on a musical performance. Similarly, drawing and painting can serve as a starting point for storytelling and role-playing.

In addition to these strategies, parents and caregivers should recognize and celebrate the value of imaginative play. Understanding that play is a crucial aspect of learning and development helps adults appreciate the importance of providing time and space for children to engage in these activities. Praising children's creativity and acknowledging their imaginative efforts reinforces the value of play and encourages them to continue exploring their imagination.

In conclusion, encouraging imaginative play is vital for children's development, as it nurtures creativity, cognitive growth, emotional regulation, and social skills. By providing open-ended toys and materials, creating a conducive environment, participating in play, and incorporating storytelling and outdoor activities, parents and caregivers can support and enrich children's imaginative experiences. Recognizing the value of imaginative play and celebrating children's creativity fosters a love for learning and exploration, laying the foundation for lifelong growth and development. Through imaginative play, children not only entertain themselves but also develop essential skills that will serve them throughout their lives.

ppp

"Encouraging a child's curiosity through questions
is like planting seeds in fertile soil. Each question
leads to new discoveries. With every answer, their
understanding of the world deepens."

ϷϷϷ

FOUR

ART AND CRAFT ACTIVITIES

Art and craft activities are vital components of a child's development, offering numerous benefits that extend beyond mere entertainment. These activities are instrumental in fostering creativity, enhancing fine motor skills, boosting cognitive development, and providing emotional and social benefits. Engaging in art and craft activities allows children to explore their imagination, express their thoughts and feelings, and develop a wide range of skills that are crucial for their overall growth.

One of the most significant benefits of art and craft activities is the enhancement of creativity. When children are given the freedom to create, they learn to think imaginatively and explore new ideas. Art provides a platform where there are no right or wrong answers, allowing children to experiment without fear of making mistakes. This freedom encourages them to take risks, try different approaches, and think outside the box. Whether they are drawing, painting, sculpting, or crafting, children use their creativity to bring their ideas to life. This creative thinking is not only beneficial for artistic pursuits but also for problem-solving and innovation in other areas of life.

Art and craft activities also play a crucial role in developing fine motor skills. As children manipulate various tools and materials, such as scissors, paintbrushes, glue, and clay, they refine their hand-eye coordination and dexterity. Cutting, pasting, drawing, and molding require precise movements and control, which help strengthen the muscles in their hands and fingers. These skills are essential for many everyday tasks, such as writing, tying shoelaces, and using utensils. By regularly engaging in art and craft activities, children develop the fine motor skills necessary for success in both academic and non-academic pursuits.

In addition to fine motor skills, art and craft activities contribute to cognitive development. When children engage in these activities, they learn to plan and organize their thoughts, follow instructions, and make decisions. For instance, deciding what colors to use, how to arrange different elements, and what materials to choose all involve cognitive processes such as critical thinking and problem-solving. These activities also enhance memory and concentration, as children need to remember steps and stay focused on their tasks. Moreover, art projects often require children to think spatially and understand concepts such as shapes, sizes, and proportions, which are fundamental for mathematical and scientific reasoning.

Emotionally, art and craft activities provide children with a valuable outlet for self-expression. Through their creations, children can convey their thoughts, feelings, and experiences, which can be especially important for those who may struggle with verbal communication. Art allows them to explore and process their emotions in a safe and non-judgmental environment. For example, a child who feels sad or anxious might use darker colors or create abstract forms to represent their feelings. This process of expressing and externalizing emotions through art can be therapeutic, helping children to understand and manage their emotions better. Additionally, the act of creating something can be a source of pride and accomplishment, boosting self-esteem and confidence.

Art and craft activities also offer social benefits, particularly when children engage in these activities with others. Collaborative art projects, such as group murals or community sculptures, teach children the importance of teamwork and cooperation. They learn to share materials, take turns, and contribute to a common goal. These social interactions help develop communication skills and foster a sense of belonging and community. Furthermore, discussing their artwork with peers or adults can enhance language skills and promote meaningful conversations. Children learn to articulate their ideas, describe their creative process, and give and receive feedback, all of which are important social competencies.

For parents and caregivers, facilitating art and craft activities at home involves providing a variety of materials and opportunities for creative exploration. Stocking up on basic art supplies, such as paper, crayons, markers, paints, glue, and scissors, ensures that children have the tools they need to engage in these activities. It's also beneficial to include a range of materials that can spark creativity, such as colored pencils, watercolors, clay, fabric scraps, beads, and recycled items. Having these materials readily accessible encourages children to initiate and engage in art projects independently.

Creating a dedicated space for art and craft activities can further enhance the experience. This space doesn't need to be elaborate; a simple table or a corner of a room where children can work on their projects is sufficient. The key is to make it an inviting and organized area where children feel free to create without worrying about making a mess. Having storage solutions, such as bins or shelves, to keep materials organized and within reach can make it easier for children to find what they need and clean up afterward.

Parents and caregivers can also actively participate in art and craft activities to support and inspire children. Engaging in these activities together can strengthen the parent-child bond and provide opportunities for shared experiences and memories. When adults model creativity and enthusiasm for art, it encourages children to explore their own creativity. Asking open-ended questions about their artwork, offering positive feedback, and showing genuine interest in their creative process can make a significant impact on a child's confidence and motivation. However, it's important to strike a balance between guiding the activity and allowing the child to take the lead. Giving children the autonomy to make their own choices and decisions fosters independence and a sense of ownership over their creations.

Incorporating art and craft activities into daily routines can also be beneficial. Simple projects, such as drawing during free time, making homemade cards for special occasions, or creating decorations for the home, can seamlessly integrate creativity into everyday life. These activities do not need to be time-consuming or complex; even a few minutes of creative engagement can have a positive impact. Additionally, finding inspiration from everyday experiences, such as nature walks, family outings, or favorite stories, can provide fresh ideas for art projects.

Art and craft activities can also be used as a tool for learning and exploring different subjects. For instance, creating a diorama of a historical event, building a model of the solar system, or making a collage of animals and their habitats can enhance understanding and retention of academic concepts. Integrating art into subjects such as science, history, and literature makes learning more engaging and interactive. It allows children to explore and express their understanding in a creative and hands-on manner, which can deepen their comprehension and interest in the subject matter.

Furthermore, art and craft activities can introduce children to different cultures and traditions, fostering cultural awareness and appreciation. Exploring art forms from various cultures, such as traditional painting techniques, folk crafts, or indigenous art, can broaden children's horizons and expose them to diverse perspectives. Celebrating cultural festivals through art projects, such as making Diwali lanterns, Chinese New Year dragons, or Native American dreamcatchers, helps children understand and appreciate the richness and diversity of the world around them.

In today's digital age, balancing screen time with hands-on creative activities is essential. While technology offers valuable tools for creativity, it's important to ensure that children have ample opportunities for physical and tactile experiences. Art and craft activities engage multiple senses and provide a break from the screen, promoting physical movement, sensory exploration, and a connection with the tangible world. Encouraging outdoor art projects, such as painting in nature, creating land art, or using natural materials for crafts, can further enhance this connection and inspire creativity through the beauty of the natural environment.

Art and craft activities are fundamental to a child's development, offering a multitude of benefits that extend beyond mere entertainment. These activities enhance creativity, fine motor skills, cognitive development, emotional expression, and social interaction. By providing a variety of materials, creating a conducive environment, participating in activities, and incorporating art into daily routines and learning, parents and caregivers can foster a love for creativity and exploration. Art and craft activities not only allow children to express themselves and develop essential skills but also provide a foundation for lifelong learning, curiosity, and appreciation for the world around them. Through these activities, children can explore their imagination, build confidence, and experience the joy of creating something uniquely their own.

ppp

"Celebrating a child's creative achievements boosts their confidence and ignites their passion. Recognition is a powerful motivator. It inspires them to pursue their dreams with even greater determination."

FIVE

MUSIC AND MOVEMENT

Music and movement are integral to a child's development, offering a wealth of benefits that encompass physical, cognitive, emotional, and social growth. These activities are not only enjoyable but also provide essential opportunities for children to explore their creativity, express themselves, and develop a range of important skills. The combination of music and movement creates a dynamic and engaging environment that can significantly enhance a child's overall development.

One of the most obvious benefits of music and movement is the development of physical skills. Movement activities, such as dancing, jumping, clapping, and swaying, help children develop their gross motor skills. These activities require coordination, balance, and spatial awareness, all of which are crucial for physical development. Dancing to music, in particular, encourages children to move their bodies in a variety of ways, enhancing their flexibility, strength, and endurance. These physical benefits extend beyond the development of motor skills; regular physical activity through music and movement also promotes overall health and well-being, helping to establish healthy habits from an early age.

In addition to gross motor skills, music and movement activities also enhance fine motor skills. Actions such as playing musical instruments, fingerplays, and hand clapping games involve precise movements that strengthen the small muscles in the hands and fingers. These activities require coordination and control, which are essential for tasks such as writing, drawing, and using utensils. By engaging in music and movement activities, children develop the fine motor skills necessary for academic and everyday tasks.

Cognitively, music and movement play a significant role in enhancing brain development. Research has shown that music stimulates various areas of the brain, including those responsible for language, memory, and spatial-temporal skills. When children listen to music, sing songs, and move to rhythms, they are engaging multiple areas of their brain simultaneously. This stimulation helps to create and strengthen neural connections, promoting cognitive flexibility and enhancing overall brain function.

Music, in particular, has a profound impact on language development. Singing songs and rhymes exposes children to a rich vocabulary and diverse sentence structures, enhancing their language skills. The repetitive and rhythmic nature of songs helps children remember words and phrases, aiding in vocabulary acquisition and language comprehension. Additionally, singing encourages children to articulate words clearly and practice their pronunciation, which is crucial for developing verbal communication skills. Music also supports the development of listening skills, as children learn to pay attention to different sounds, rhythms, and melodies.

Movement activities further contribute to cognitive development by promoting problem-solving and critical thinking skills. When children engage in movement activities, they often need to follow instructions, remember sequences, and make decisions about how to move their bodies. These tasks require cognitive processes such as planning, organizing, and executing actions, which are essential for problem-solving and critical thinking. Additionally, movement activities often involve patterns and sequences, which help children develop an understanding of mathematical concepts such as counting, symmetry, and spatial relationships.

Emotionally, music and movement provide children with a valuable outlet for self-expression and emotional regulation. Music has the power to evoke a wide range of emotions, and through music, children can explore and express their feelings in a safe and supportive environment. Singing, dancing, and playing instruments allow children to convey their emotions, whether they are happy, sad, excited, or frustrated. This process of expressing emotions through music helps children to understand and manage their feelings, promoting emotional regulation and resilience.

Movement activities also play a crucial role in emotional development by helping children to release pent-up energy and stress. Physical activity through movement can be a great way for children to cope with feelings of anxiety or frustration. Dancing, for example, provides a joyful and energetic outlet for children to release their emotions and boost their mood. The physical exertion involved in movement activities also triggers the release of endorphins, which are natural mood enhancers, promoting a sense of well-being and happiness.

Socially, music and movement activities offer numerous opportunities for interaction and collaboration. Group music activities, such as singing in a choir, playing in an ensemble, or participating in music classes, teach children the importance of teamwork and cooperation. These activities require children to listen to each other, follow a conductor or leader, and work together to create harmonious sounds. Through these interactions, children develop important social skills such as communication, empathy, and respect for others.

Movement activities, such as dance classes, group games, and physical play, also promote social interaction and cooperation. When children engage in movement activities with others, they learn to take turns, share space, and collaborate to achieve common goals. These social interactions help children develop a sense of community and belonging, which are essential for building and maintaining healthy relationships.

For parents and caregivers, facilitating music and movement activities at home involves providing a variety of opportunities and resources. Incorporating music into daily routines can be as simple as playing songs during playtime, singing lullabies at bedtime, or having a family dance party. Exposing children to different genres of music, such as classical, jazz, folk, and world music, broadens their musical horizons and introduces them to diverse cultural traditions. Providing musical instruments, such as drums, tambourines, xylophones, and maracas, allows children to explore different sounds and create their own music.

Creating a conducive environment for movement activities is equally important. Providing space for children to move freely and engage in physical play encourages them to be active and explore their movement abilities. Simple equipment such as mats, hula hoops, and ribbons can add variety and fun to movement activities. Encouraging outdoor play, such as running, jumping, climbing, and playing sports, further enhances physical development and promotes a connection with nature.

Parents and caregivers can also actively participate in music and movement activities to support and inspire children. Singing songs, dancing, and playing instruments together can create joyful and meaningful shared experiences. These activities not only strengthen the parent-child bond but also provide opportunities for parents to model musicality and movement. Participating in group music and movement classes, such as mommy-and-me music sessions or family dance workshops, can offer additional social and developmental benefits.

Incorporating music and movement into learning activities can further enhance children's development. For example, using songs and rhymes to teach concepts such as the alphabet, numbers, and colors makes learning more engaging and memorable. Movement activities, such as action songs and dance routines, can reinforce academic concepts and improve retention. Integrating music and movement into subjects such as science, history, and literature provides a multisensory approach to learning, making it more dynamic and interactive.

Music and movement also provide valuable opportunities for creative expression and exploration. Encouraging children to compose their own songs, create dance routines, or experiment with different instruments fosters creativity and innovation. These activities allow children to explore their interests, develop their unique talents, and express their individuality. Celebrating children's musical and movement creations, whether through performances, recordings, or informal family gatherings, boosts their confidence and reinforces the value of their creative efforts.

Furthermore, music and movement activities can introduce children to different cultures and traditions, fostering cultural awareness and appreciation. Exploring music and dance from various cultures exposes children to diverse rhythms, melodies, and movements, broadening their understanding of the world. Participating in cultural festivals, attending performances, and learning traditional songs and dances can enrich children's cultural experiences and promote a sense of global citizenship.

In conclusion, music and movement are essential components of a child's development, offering a wide range of physical, cognitive, emotional, and social benefits. These activities enhance motor skills, stimulate brain development, support language acquisition, and promote emotional expression and regulation. They also provide valuable opportunities for social interaction, teamwork, and cultural exploration. By providing a variety of resources, creating a conducive environment, and actively participating in music and movement activities, parents and caregivers can foster a love for creativity, exploration, and lifelong learning. Through the joyful and dynamic experiences of music and movement, children can develop essential skills, build confidence, and experience the profound benefits of creative expression.

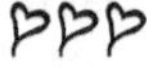

"Supporting individual interests helps children develop a sense of identity and purpose. It allows them to explore their passions deeply. This personalized approach to learning is the foundation of lifelong growth."

ᗞᗞᗞ

SIX

STORYTELLING AND CREATIVE WRITING

Storytelling and creative writing are foundational activities that play a crucial role in the development of children. These practices offer a multitude of benefits, including enhancing language skills, stimulating imagination, fostering emotional growth, and promoting cognitive and social development. Through storytelling and creative writing, children learn to express themselves, understand the world around them, and develop a love for literature and communication.

One of the primary benefits of storytelling and creative writing is the enhancement of language skills. Engaging in these activities helps children develop a rich vocabulary and an understanding of sentence structure and grammar. When children listen to stories, they are exposed to new words and phrases, which they can then incorporate into their own speech and writing. Storytelling also introduces children to different narrative styles and literary devices, such as metaphors, similes, and personification, enriching their language comprehension. By creating their own stories, children practice using language creatively and effectively, improving their ability to articulate thoughts and ideas.

Storytelling and creative writing stimulate children's imagination and creativity. When children listen to or create stories, they enter worlds of their own making, populated by characters and scenarios born from their imagination. This process of imagining and constructing narratives helps children develop creative thinking skills. They learn to generate original ideas, explore different perspectives, and think critically about plot development and character motivation. Creative writing, in particular, allows children to experiment with different genres and styles, from fantasy and science fiction to poetry and drama, further expanding their creative horizons.

Emotionally, storytelling and creative writing provide children with valuable outlets for self-expression and emotional exploration. Through the characters and events in their stories, children can explore and process their own feelings and experiences. Writing about personal experiences or creating fictional scenarios that mirror their emotions allows children to externalize and make sense of their feelings. This process of emotional expression and exploration is crucial for developing emotional intelligence and resilience. It helps children understand and manage their emotions, reducing anxiety and promoting mental well-being.

Storytelling and creative writing also contribute to cognitive development by enhancing critical thinking and problem-solving skills. Crafting a story requires children to plan and organize their thoughts, develop a coherent narrative structure, and resolve conflicts within the plot. These tasks involve cognitive processes such as sequencing, cause-and-effect reasoning, and logical thinking. Additionally, creative writing often requires children to conduct research and gather information to create believable settings and characters, further enhancing their cognitive abilities. The process of editing and revising their work teaches children to evaluate and improve their writing, fostering a growth mindset and attention to detail.

Socially, storytelling and creative writing offer opportunities for collaboration and communication. When children share their stories with others, whether through oral storytelling, written compositions, or group projects, they develop important social skills. They learn to listen to others, give and receive feedback, and appreciate different viewpoints. Collaborative storytelling activities, such as group storytelling games or co-authoring a story, teach children to work together, negotiate ideas, and build on each other's contributions. These social interactions help children develop empathy, cooperation, and a sense of community.

For parents and caregivers, encouraging storytelling and creative writing at home involves providing a supportive and stimulating environment. Reading to children regularly is one of the most effective ways to foster a love for storytelling and literature. By exposing children to a wide range of stories, from fairy tales and fables to contemporary fiction and non-fiction, parents can ignite their curiosity and imagination. Discussing the stories and asking open-ended questions about the characters, plot, and themes can further enhance children's understanding and engagement.

Creating a dedicated space for writing and storytelling can also encourage children to explore these activities. A quiet, comfortable area with access to writing materials, such as notebooks, pens, pencils, and art supplies, provides children with the tools they need to create their own stories. Encouraging children to keep a journal or diary can help them develop a regular writing habit and provide a personal space for self-expression.

Parents and caregivers can also participate in storytelling and creative writing activities with children. Telling stories together, whether through bedtime stories, family storytelling sessions, or storytelling games, can create joyful and meaningful shared experiences. These activities not only strengthen the parent-child bond but also model storytelling techniques and inspire children's own creative efforts. Encouraging children to write their own stories and share them with family members can boost their confidence and sense of accomplishment.

Incorporating storytelling and creative writing into everyday activities can further enhance children's engagement and enjoyment. Simple activities, such as creating stories based on daily experiences, writing letters or postcards to friends and family, or making up stories about favorite toys and characters, can make storytelling and writing a natural and enjoyable part of daily life. Encouraging children to draw pictures and then write stories about their drawings combines visual and verbal creativity, providing a multisensory approach to storytelling.

Technology can also be a valuable tool for storytelling and creative writing. Digital storytelling apps, writing software, and online platforms for sharing stories offer new and exciting ways for children to create and share their work. These tools can enhance children's writing skills by providing interactive and multimedia elements, such as adding images, sounds, and animations to their stories. However, it's important to balance screen time with traditional writing and storytelling activities to ensure a well-rounded creative experience.

Storytelling and creative writing can also be used as educational tools to enhance learning across different subjects. For example, writing historical fiction stories can deepen children's understanding of historical events and figures, while creating science fiction stories can spark interest in scientific concepts and discoveries. Using storytelling to explore mathematical problems or create stories about mathematical adventures can make learning math more engaging and accessible. Integrating creative writing into subjects such as social studies, science, and literature allows children to explore and express their understanding in creative and meaningful ways.

Encouraging children to read a variety of genres and styles can further enrich their storytelling and writing skills. Exposing children to poetry, plays, myths, legends, and contemporary fiction broadens their literary horizons and introduces them to different narrative techniques and literary traditions. Discussing the structure, themes, and styles of different genres helps children develop a deeper appreciation for literature and inspires them to experiment with their own writing.

Celebrating children's storytelling and creative writing efforts is crucial for fostering a love for these activities. Displaying their written work, creating family storybooks, or organizing storytelling events where children can share their stories with others can boost their confidence and motivation. Recognizing and praising their creativity, effort, and improvement reinforces the value of storytelling and writing and encourages them to continue exploring their creative potential.

Storytelling and creative writing also offer valuable opportunities for cultural exploration and appreciation. Sharing stories from different cultures and traditions exposes children to diverse perspectives and experiences, promoting cultural awareness and empathy. Encouraging children to create stories based on their own cultural heritage or incorporating elements from different cultures into their writing can deepen their understanding of and appreciation for cultural diversity.

Storytelling and creative writing are essential activities that offer a multitude of benefits for children's development. These activities enhance language skills, stimulate imagination and creativity, foster emotional growth, and promote cognitive and social development. By providing a supportive and stimulating environment, participating in storytelling and writing activities, and incorporating these practices into everyday life, parents and caregivers can nurture a love for literature and communication in children. Through storytelling and creative writing, children can explore their imagination, express their thoughts and feelings, and develop the skills and confidence needed for lifelong learning and growth.

ppp

"Creative challenges and competitions provide valuable learning experiences. They teach children the importance of effort and perseverance. These activities also foster a spirit of healthy competition and camaraderie."

❦❦❦

SEVEN

NATURE AND OUTDOOR EXPLORATION

Nature and outdoor exploration are fundamental to a child's development, providing a rich and dynamic environment where children can learn, grow, and thrive. These activities offer myriad benefits, including physical, cognitive, emotional, and social growth. Spending time outdoors and engaging with nature allows children to explore the natural world, fostering a sense of wonder and curiosity that is essential for lifelong learning.

One of the most significant benefits of nature and outdoor exploration is the development of physical skills. Outdoor activities such as running, climbing, jumping, and playing sports help children develop their gross motor skills, improving their strength, coordination, and balance. These activities require children to use their whole bodies, promoting overall physical fitness and health. Additionally, the varied terrain and natural obstacles found in outdoor environments challenge children's physical abilities, encouraging them to push their limits and develop resilience. Regular physical activity is crucial for maintaining a healthy weight, building strong muscles and bones, and reducing the risk of chronic diseases such as obesity and diabetes.

In addition to gross motor skills, nature and outdoor exploration enhance fine motor skills. Activities such as picking flowers, collecting rocks, building sandcastles, and drawing in the dirt require precise movements and hand-eye coordination. These activities help strengthen the small muscles in the hands and fingers, which are essential for tasks such as writing, drawing, and using tools. Engaging in these activities regularly helps children develop the fine motor skills necessary for success in both academic and everyday tasks.

Cognitively, nature and outdoor exploration play a significant role in enhancing brain development. The natural environment provides a wealth of sensory experiences that stimulate the brain and promote cognitive growth. The sights, sounds, smells, and textures of nature engage children's senses, helping them develop sensory awareness and processing skills. For example, listening to the sound of birds singing, feeling the texture of tree bark, and observing the colors and shapes of flowers all contribute to sensory development. These sensory experiences are crucial for brain development, as they help create and strengthen neural connections.

Nature and outdoor exploration also support cognitive development by promoting problem-solving and critical thinking skills. When children explore the outdoors, they encounter a variety of challenges and opportunities that require them to think creatively and make decisions. For example, navigating a hiking trail, building a shelter, or identifying different plants and animals all involve cognitive processes such as observation, analysis, and evaluation. These activities encourage children to think independently, develop hypotheses, test their ideas, and learn from their experiences. Additionally, the natural environment provides opportunities for unstructured play and exploration, which are essential for fostering creativity and innovation.

Emotionally, nature and outdoor exploration provide children with valuable opportunities for self-expression and emotional regulation. Spending time outdoors allows children to experience a sense of freedom and autonomy, which can boost their confidence and self-esteem. The natural environment also provides a calming and restorative setting that can help reduce stress and anxiety. For example, spending time in a forest, by a river, or in a garden can have a soothing effect on the mind and body, promoting relaxation and well-being. Additionally, outdoor activities such as hiking, camping, and gardening provide opportunities for children to set and achieve personal goals, which can foster a sense of accomplishment and pride.

Socially, nature and outdoor exploration offer numerous opportunities for interaction and collaboration. Group activities such as team sports, group hikes, and nature-based games teach children the importance of teamwork and cooperation. These activities require children to communicate effectively, share resources, and work together to achieve common goals. Through these social interactions, children develop important social skills such as empathy, cooperation, and conflict resolution. Additionally, spending time outdoors with family and friends provides opportunities for bonding and creating lasting memories.

For parents and caregivers, facilitating nature and outdoor exploration involves providing opportunities and resources for children to engage with the natural environment. Encouraging children to spend time outdoors and explore their surroundings can be as simple as taking regular walks in the park, visiting nature reserves, or spending time in the backyard. Providing tools and materials such as magnifying glasses, binoculars, field guides, and nature journals can enhance children's exploration and learning experiences. These tools can help children observe and document their findings, deepening their understanding and appreciation of the natural world.

Creating a conducive environment for nature and outdoor exploration also involves ensuring children's safety while allowing them the freedom to explore. Supervising children and setting boundaries are important for preventing accidents and injuries. However, it's also essential to give children the autonomy to take risks and learn from their experiences. Allowing children to climb trees, navigate uneven terrain, and explore natural features such as streams and rocks can help them develop confidence and resilience. Providing guidance and support while encouraging independence fosters a sense of adventure and curiosity.

Parents and caregivers can also actively participate in nature and outdoor exploration activities with children. Engaging in these activities together can create meaningful shared experiences and strengthen the parent-child bond. Activities such as hiking, camping, birdwatching, and gardening provide opportunities for family members to connect with each other and with nature. Participating in nature-based activities can also model positive behaviors and attitudes towards the natural environment, inspiring children to develop a lifelong appreciation for nature.

Incorporating nature and outdoor exploration into everyday activities can further enhance children's engagement and enjoyment. Simple activities such as planting a garden, creating a nature scavenger hunt, or building a birdhouse can make nature and outdoor exploration a natural and enjoyable part of daily life. These activities do not need to be time-consuming or complex; even a few minutes of outdoor play and exploration can have a positive impact. Additionally, finding inspiration from everyday experiences, such as observing the changing seasons, watching wildlife, or collecting natural treasures, can provide fresh ideas for outdoor activities.

Educationally, nature and outdoor exploration can be used as powerful tools for learning and discovery. The natural environment provides a rich and dynamic classroom where children can explore and learn about a wide range of subjects, from biology and ecology to geography and astronomy. For example, observing the life cycle of plants and animals, studying weather patterns, and exploring geological formations can deepen children's understanding of scientific concepts and phenomena. Using nature as a context for learning makes education more engaging and relevant, fostering a sense of wonder and curiosity about the world.

Nature and outdoor exploration also provide valuable opportunities for cultural and historical learning. Exploring natural landscapes, historical sites, and cultural landmarks can deepen children's understanding of their heritage and the world around them. Learning about indigenous plants and animals, traditional practices, and historical events connected to natural sites can foster a sense of cultural awareness and appreciation. Participating in cultural festivals, attending outdoor performances, and visiting heritage sites can enrich children's cultural experiences and promote a sense of global citizenship.

In today's digital age, balancing screen time with nature and outdoor exploration is essential for children's development. While technology offers valuable tools for learning and entertainment, it's important to ensure that children have ample opportunities for physical and tactile experiences in the natural environment. Engaging with nature provides a break from screens and promotes physical movement, sensory exploration, and a connection with the tangible world. Encouraging outdoor activities such as hiking, gardening, and playing in natural settings can enhance children's overall well-being and foster a sense of environmental stewardship.

Celebrating children's nature and outdoor exploration efforts is crucial for fostering a love for these activities. Recognizing and praising their curiosity, effort, and discoveries reinforces the value of nature and outdoor exploration and encourages them to continue exploring the natural world. Creating nature journals, sharing stories about outdoor adventures, and displaying collections of natural treasures can boost children's confidence and motivation. These activities also provide opportunities for reflection and learning, helping children to develop a deeper understanding and appreciation of the natural environment.

In conclusion, nature and outdoor exploration are essential activities that offer a multitude of benefits for children's development. These activities enhance physical skills, stimulate cognitive growth, support emotional well-being, and promote social interaction. By providing opportunities and resources for nature and outdoor exploration, creating a conducive environment, and participating in these activities with children, parents and caregivers can foster a love for nature and lifelong learning. Through the rich and dynamic experiences of nature and outdoor exploration, children can develop essential skills, build confidence, and experience the profound benefits of connecting with the natural world.

ᐅᐅᐅ

"Exploring different cultures broadens a child's horizons and fosters empathy. It helps them appreciate the richness of human diversity. This understanding is crucial for developing global citizens."

▷▷▷

EIGHT

BUILDING AND CONSTRUCTION PLAY

Building and construction play are critical components of childhood development, offering numerous benefits that extend across physical, cognitive, emotional, and social domains. These activities, which involve manipulating materials to create structures, offer children opportunities to explore their creativity, solve problems, and develop a range of essential skills. Engaging in building and construction play not only entertains children but also lays the foundation for their learning and growth.

One of the primary benefits of building and construction play is the development of fine motor skills. Activities such as stacking blocks, connecting LEGO pieces, and assembling construction sets require precise movements and hand-eye coordination. These actions strengthen the small muscles in the hands and fingers, which are crucial for tasks such as writing, drawing, and using tools. By regularly engaging in building and construction play, children develop the dexterity and control necessary for success in both academic and everyday activities.

In addition to fine motor skills, building and construction play also enhance gross motor skills. Larger construction activities, such as building forts, creating obstacle courses, or using large foam blocks, involve whole-body movements. These activities require children to lift, carry, balance, and coordinate their movements, promoting overall physical fitness and health. Engaging in these activities helps children develop their strength, coordination, and spatial awareness, which are essential for physical development.

Cognitively, building and construction play play a significant role in enhancing problem-solving and critical thinking skills. When children engage in these activities, they are often presented with challenges that require them to think creatively and analytically. For example, deciding how to balance blocks to create a stable structure, figuring out how to connect pieces to build a specific design, or solving problems that arise during construction all involve cognitive processes such as planning, reasoning, and evaluating. These activities encourage children to experiment with different solutions, learn from their mistakes, and develop resilience and perseverance.

Building and construction play also support cognitive development by promoting spatial reasoning and mathematical skills. Creating structures requires children to understand concepts such as shapes, sizes, proportions, and symmetry. These activities help children develop their spatial awareness and ability to visualize and manipulate objects in three-dimensional space. Additionally, building and construction play often involve counting, measuring, and comparing, which reinforce mathematical concepts such as numbers, geometry, and measurement. By engaging in these activities, children develop a strong foundation for later learning in science, technology, engineering, and mathematics (STEM).

Emotionally, building and construction play provide children with valuable opportunities for self-expression and emotional regulation. Creating structures allows children to bring their ideas and imagination to life, providing a sense of accomplishment and pride. This process of creation and expression can boost children's self-esteem and confidence. Additionally, building and construction play offer opportunities for children to set and achieve goals, which can foster a sense of purpose and motivation. The focus and concentration required for these activities can also provide a calming and therapeutic effect, helping children to manage stress and anxiety.

Socially, building and construction play offer numerous opportunities for interaction and collaboration. Group activities, such as building a fort together, participating in a LEGO club, or working on a collaborative construction project, teach children the importance of teamwork and cooperation. These activities require children to communicate effectively, share materials, take turns, and work together to achieve a common goal. Through these social interactions, children develop important social skills such as empathy, cooperation, and conflict resolution. Additionally, discussing their creations and explaining their thought processes to others can enhance children's language and communication skills.

For parents and caregivers, facilitating building and construction play involves providing a variety of materials and opportunities for creative exploration. Offering a range of building materials, such as wooden blocks, LEGO sets, construction toys, and recycled materials, ensures that children have the tools they need to engage in these activities. Providing open-ended materials, such as cardboard boxes, craft sticks, and clay, encourages children to use their imagination and creativity to create their own designs.

Creating a conducive environment for building and construction play also involves setting aside time and space for these activities. Designating a specific area for building and construction play, such as a corner of a room or a dedicated playroom, can help children focus and engage in their activities without distractions. Ensuring that the space is safe and organized, with easy access to materials, can make it easier for children to initiate and sustain their play. Additionally, providing opportunities for both independent and collaborative play allows children to explore their creativity and develop their skills in different contexts.

Parents and caregivers can also actively participate in building and construction play to support and inspire children. Engaging in these activities together can create joyful and meaningful shared experiences and strengthen the parent-child bond. By building and creating together, parents can model problem-solving techniques, introduce new ideas, and provide gentle guidance. Asking open-ended questions about children's creations, offering positive feedback, and showing genuine interest in their creative process can make a significant impact on a child's confidence and motivation. However, it's important to strike a balance between guiding the activity and allowing the child to take the lead. Giving children the autonomy to make their own choices and decisions fosters independence and a sense of ownership over their creations.

Incorporating building and construction play into everyday activities can further enhance children's engagement and enjoyment. Simple activities, such as building structures with household items, creating DIY projects, or designing and constructing models, can make building and construction play a natural and enjoyable part of daily life. These activities do not need to be time-consuming or complex; even a few minutes of building and construction play can have a positive impact. Additionally, finding inspiration from everyday experiences, such as constructing models of favorite places, designing inventions, or building replicas of real-world structures, can provide fresh ideas for play.

Educationally, building and construction play can be used as powerful tools for learning and discovery. Integrating these activities into subjects such as science, technology, engineering, and mathematics (STEM) can make learning more engaging and relevant. For example, building a model bridge can teach children about engineering principles, constructing a simple machine can introduce them to physics concepts, and creating a scale model can enhance their understanding of measurement and proportions. Using building and construction play to explore academic concepts makes education more interactive and hands-on, fostering a love for learning and curiosity about the world.

Building and construction play also offer valuable opportunities for cultural and historical learning. Exploring different architectural styles, learning about famous structures and landmarks, and understanding traditional building techniques can deepen children's appreciation for cultural diversity and heritage. Participating in projects such as creating models of historical buildings, designing structures inspired by different cultures, or constructing replicas of famous landmarks can enrich children's cultural experiences and promote a sense of global citizenship.

In today's digital age, balancing screen time with hands-on building and construction play is essential for children's development. While technology offers valuable tools for learning and creativity, it's important to ensure that children have ample opportunities for physical and tactile experiences. Engaging in building and construction play provides a break from screens and promotes physical movement, sensory exploration, and a connection with the tangible world. Encouraging outdoor building activities, such as constructing forts, creating natural sculptures, or building with natural materials, can enhance this connection and inspire creativity through the beauty of the natural environment.

Celebrating children's building and construction play efforts is crucial for fostering a love for these activities. Recognizing and praising their creativity, effort, and problem-solving skills reinforces the value of building and construction play and encourages them to continue exploring their creativity. Creating displays of children's creations, sharing stories about their building projects, and organizing events where children can showcase their work can boost their confidence and motivation. These activities also provide opportunities for reflection and learning, helping children to develop a deeper understanding and appreciation of the building and construction process.

Building and construction play are essential activities that offer a multitude of benefits for children's development. These activities enhance fine and gross motor skills, stimulate cognitive growth, support emotional well-being, and promote social interaction. By providing a variety of materials and opportunities for creative exploration, creating a conducive environment, and participating in these activities with children, parents and caregivers can foster a love for building and construction play and lifelong learning. Through the rich and dynamic experiences of building and construction play, children can develop essential skills, build confidence, and experience the profound benefits of creative expression.

"Nature and outdoor exploration stimulate a child's senses and inspire wonder. The natural world is a dynamic playground for learning. Time spent in nature fosters a lifelong love for the environment."

♥♥♥

NINE

CREATIVE PROBLEM-SOLVING SKILLS

Creative problem-solving skills are essential for navigating the complexities of life and achieving success in various domains. These skills enable individuals to approach challenges with innovative thinking, adaptability, and a willingness to explore multiple solutions. For children, developing creative problem-solving skills is particularly important as it fosters cognitive growth, enhances emotional resilience, and prepares them for future academic and professional endeavors. Engaging in activities that promote creative problem-solving helps children become confident, resourceful, and effective thinkers.

One of the key components of creative problem-solving is the ability to think divergently. Divergent thinking involves generating a wide range of ideas and exploring different possibilities before converging on a single solution. This type of thinking encourages children to move beyond conventional approaches and consider alternative perspectives. Activities that promote divergent thinking, such as brainstorming sessions, open-ended questions, and creative challenges, help children develop their ability to think outside the box. For example, asking children to come up with multiple uses for a common object, such as a paperclip, encourages them to think creatively and consider various possibilities.

Encouraging curiosity and a sense of wonder is also crucial for fostering creative problem-solving skills. Children who are curious and inquisitive are more likely to explore new ideas and seek out novel solutions. Parents and caregivers can nurture curiosity by providing opportunities for exploration and discovery. This can involve exposing children to a wide range of experiences, such as visiting museums, exploring nature, and engaging in hands-on activities. Asking open-ended questions and encouraging children to ask their own questions can further stimulate their curiosity and drive to learn.

Creative problem-solving also requires the ability to think critically and analytically. Critical thinking involves evaluating information, identifying patterns, and making connections between different concepts. Activities that promote critical thinking, such as puzzles, games, and logic challenges, help children develop their analytical skills. For example, solving a jigsaw puzzle requires children to analyze the shapes and colors of pieces, identify patterns, and determine how they fit together. Similarly, playing strategy games, such as chess or board games, encourages children to think ahead, anticipate potential outcomes, and develop strategic plans.

Another important aspect of creative problem-solving is the willingness to take risks and embrace failure. Children who are afraid of making mistakes or experiencing failure may be hesitant to try new approaches or explore unconventional solutions. Encouraging a growth mindset, which emphasizes the value of effort and learning from mistakes, can help children develop resilience and a positive attitude toward challenges. Parents and caregivers can model a growth mindset by praising effort and perseverance rather than focusing solely on outcomes. Sharing stories of successful individuals who overcame obstacles and learned from their failures can also inspire children to view challenges as opportunities for growth.

Collaboration and teamwork are also essential for developing creative problem-solving skills. Working with others allows children to share ideas, gain new perspectives, and build on each other's strengths. Collaborative activities, such as group projects, team sports, and cooperative games, teach children the importance of communication, cooperation, and compromise. These experiences help children develop their ability to work effectively with others, listen to different viewpoints, and negotiate solutions. For example, participating in a group project where children must work together to build a model or complete a task requires them to collaborate, delegate responsibilities, and integrate their ideas.

Providing opportunities for hands-on, experiential learning is another effective way to promote creative problem-solving skills. Hands-on activities, such as building projects, science experiments, and art projects, allow children to explore concepts in a tangible and interactive way. These activities encourage experimentation, trial and error, and iterative thinking. For example, conducting a science experiment where children must design and test their hypotheses involves multiple stages of problem-solving, from planning and executing the experiment to analyzing the results and drawing conclusions. Similarly, building a structure with blocks or other materials requires children to experiment with different designs, identify structural weaknesses, and make adjustments to achieve stability.

Encouraging children to set goals and pursue their interests can also foster creative problem-solving skills. When children are motivated by their passions and interests, they are more likely to engage deeply with challenges and persist in finding solutions.

Parents and caregivers can support children's interests by providing resources, guidance, and encouragement. For example, if a child is interested in robotics, providing access to robotics kits, coding software, and related books can help them explore their interest and develop problem-solving skills in the process. Setting goals, such as completing a specific project or mastering a new skill, provides children with a sense of purpose and direction, motivating them to overcome obstacles and achieve their objectives.

Exposure to diverse perspectives and experiences is also important for developing creative problem-solving skills. Interacting with people from different backgrounds, cultures, and disciplines can broaden children's horizons and stimulate new ways of thinking. Encouraging children to read diverse books, engage in cultural activities, and participate in community events can provide them with a rich tapestry of experiences to draw from when solving problems. Additionally, fostering an inclusive and respectful environment where diverse viewpoints are valued and celebrated can help children develop empathy and open-mindedness, which are essential for effective problem-solving.

Reflection and self-assessment are also critical components of creative problem-solving. Encouraging children to reflect on their experiences, evaluate their approaches, and consider what they have learned helps them develop self-awareness and improve their problem-solving abilities. Reflective activities, such as journaling, discussions, and self-assessment checklists, provide opportunities for children to think critically about their problem-solving processes and identify areas for growth. For example, after completing a project, asking children to reflect on what went well, what challenges they encountered, and what they would do differently next time can help them develop a deeper understanding of their problem-solving strategies and how to improve them.

Incorporating technology and digital tools can also enhance

creative problem-solving skills. Technology provides access to a wealth of information, resources, and tools that can support problem-solving efforts. For example, using coding software to create a program or game involves logical thinking, planning, and troubleshooting. Digital tools, such as simulation software, virtual labs, and online collaboration platforms, provide interactive and engaging ways for children to explore concepts and solve problems. However, it is important to balance screen time with hands-on, real-world experiences to ensure a well-rounded development of problem-solving skills.

Parents and caregivers can play a vital role in fostering creative problem-solving skills by creating a supportive and stimulating environment. Providing a variety of materials, resources, and opportunities for exploration encourages children to engage in problem-solving activities. Creating a space where children feel safe to take risks, make mistakes, and learn from their experiences is essential for nurturing their creativity and resilience. Additionally, modeling problem-solving behaviors, such as thinking aloud, asking questions, and demonstrating perseverance, can inspire children to adopt similar approaches in their own problem-solving efforts.

Celebrating and recognizing children's problem-solving efforts and achievements is also important for fostering a love for creative problem-solving. Praising children for their creativity, effort, and persistence reinforces the value of these skills and encourages them to continue exploring and developing their problem-solving abilities. Creating opportunities for children to showcase their work, share their experiences, and receive feedback from others can boost their confidence and motivation. For example, organizing a science fair, art exhibit, or project presentation where children can present their problem-solving projects to family, friends, and the community can provide a platform for recognition and celebration.

In conclusion, creative problem-solving skills are essential for navigating the complexities of life and achieving success in various domains. These skills enable individuals to approach challenges with innovative thinking, adaptability, and a willingness to explore multiple solutions. For children, developing creative problem-solving skills is particularly important as it fosters cognitive growth, enhances emotional resilience, and prepares them for future academic and professional endeavors. By providing opportunities for divergent thinking, nurturing curiosity, promoting critical thinking, encouraging risk-taking, fostering collaboration, and supporting hands-on learning, parents and caregivers can help children develop the creative problem-solving skills they need to thrive. Through the rich and dynamic experiences of creative problem-solving, children can develop essential skills, build confidence, and experience the profound benefits of innovative thinking and effective problem-solving.

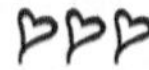

"Storytelling and creative writing are powerful tools for self-expression. They help children articulate their thoughts and emotions. These activities also enhance their language skills and cognitive development."

♥♥♥

TEN

ROLE-PLAYING AND DRAMA

Role-playing and drama are powerful tools for childhood development, offering a wealth of benefits across various domains, including cognitive, emotional, social, and linguistic growth. Engaging in these activities allows children to step into different roles and scenarios, which helps them explore different perspectives, develop empathy, and enhance their communication skills. Through role-playing and drama, children can express their creativity, navigate complex social interactions, and gain a deeper understanding of themselves and the world around them.

One of the most significant benefits of role-playing and drama is the enhancement of cognitive skills. When children engage in these activities, they use their imagination to create and inhabit different characters and scenarios. This process of imaginative play stimulates cognitive development by encouraging children to think abstractly and symbolically. They learn to construct narratives, understand cause-and-effect relationships, and make connections between different ideas. For instance, acting out a story involves understanding the plot, developing characters, and remembering dialogue, all of which require cognitive processes such as memory, attention, and planning.

Role-playing and drama also promote problem-solving and critical thinking skills. When children engage in dramatic play, they often encounter situations that require them to think on their feet and come up with creative solutions. For example, if they are pretending to be explorers lost in the jungle, they must figure out how to find their way home using their surroundings and resources. This kind of play encourages children to think divergently, exploring multiple possibilities and considering various outcomes. It also fosters resilience, as they learn to adapt to new challenges and persist in finding solutions.

Emotionally, role-playing and drama provide children with valuable opportunities for self-expression and emotional exploration. Taking on different roles allows children to explore a wide range of emotions in a safe and supportive environment. They can experiment with expressing feelings such as joy, anger, fear, and sadness through their characters. This process helps children understand and manage their own emotions better, enhancing their emotional intelligence and regulation. For example, acting out a scene where a character is feeling scared can help a child process their own fears and develop coping strategies. Additionally, role-playing and drama can be therapeutic, providing an outlet for children to release pent-up emotions and stress.

Role-playing and drama also play a crucial role in social development. Engaging in these activities requires children to interact with others, collaborate on creating scenarios, and communicate effectively. They learn to take turns, share ideas, and work together to bring their stories to life. These social interactions help children develop important social skills such as empathy, cooperation, and conflict resolution. By stepping into different roles, children learn to see things from other perspectives, which enhances their ability to understand and relate to others. For example, pretending to be a doctor treating a patient helps a child develop empathy and compassion for others' experiences.

Language and communication skills are significantly enhanced through role-playing and drama. These activities provide children with opportunities to practice and expand their vocabulary, improve their articulation, and develop their conversational skills. When children engage in dramatic play, they must communicate their ideas, negotiate roles, and express their characters' thoughts and emotions. This process helps them develop their language skills in a meaningful and engaging context. For example, playing the role of a teacher explaining a lesson to students requires a child to use clear and precise language, enhancing their verbal communication skills. Additionally, memorizing and delivering lines in a play or skit can improve children's reading fluency and comprehension.

Role-playing and drama can also be used as educational tools to enhance learning across various subjects. For example, acting out historical events or literary scenes can deepen children's understanding of history and literature. They can gain a more immersive and empathetic perspective on historical figures and events, which can make learning more engaging and memorable. Similarly, using drama to explore scientific concepts, such as acting out the life cycle of a butterfly or the water cycle, can help children grasp complex ideas in a fun and interactive way. This multisensory approach to learning makes education more dynamic and accessible, fostering a love for learning and curiosity.

Incorporating role-playing and drama into everyday activities can further enhance children's development. Parents and caregivers can encourage dramatic play by providing costumes, props, and other materials that inspire imaginative scenarios. Simple items such as hats, scarves, and household objects can be transformed into props for endless creative play. Creating a dedicated space for dramatic play, such as a corner of a room with a dress-up box and a small stage area, can provide children with a designated area to explore their creativity.

Participating in role-playing and drama activities with children can also strengthen the parent-child bond and provide valuable opportunities for shared experiences. Parents and caregivers can join in the play, taking on roles and creating stories together. This involvement not only supports children's development but also models positive social interactions and communication skills. Encouraging children to create and perform their own plays or skits for family and friends can boost their confidence and provide a platform for them to showcase their creativity.

Technology can also be a valuable tool for enhancing role-playing and drama activities. Digital storytelling apps, video recording tools, and online platforms for sharing performances offer new and exciting ways for children to create and share their work. These tools can enhance children's drama experiences by providing interactive and multimedia elements, such as adding music, sound effects, and digital backgrounds to their performances. However, it is important to balance screen time with hands-on, real-world dramatic play to ensure a well-rounded creative experience.

Role-playing and drama can also provide valuable opportunities for cultural exploration and appreciation. Exploring stories and characters from different cultures through dramatic play can broaden children's horizons and promote cultural awareness and empathy. Participating in cultural festivals, attending theatrical performances, and learning about traditional storytelling and drama techniques from various cultures can enrich children's cultural experiences and foster a sense of global citizenship.

For educators, incorporating role-playing and drama into the curriculum can make learning more engaging and effective. Using drama-based activities to explore academic content, such as reenacting historical events, performing literary scenes, or dramatizing scientific concepts, can deepen students' understanding and retention of the material. Drama activities can also be used to develop social-emotional skills, such as empathy, teamwork, and conflict resolution, by allowing students to explore different perspectives and practice positive social interactions.

Celebrating children's role-playing and drama efforts is crucial for fostering a love for these activities. Recognizing and praising their creativity, effort, and performance skills reinforces the value of dramatic play and encourages them to continue exploring their creativity. Creating opportunities for children to showcase their work, such as organizing school plays, family skits, or community performances, can boost their confidence and motivation. These events also provide a platform for children to receive feedback and appreciation from others, further enhancing their self-esteem and sense of accomplishment.

In conclusion, role-playing and drama are essential activities that offer a multitude of benefits for children's development. These activities enhance cognitive skills, promote emotional growth, support social development, and improve language and communication abilities. By providing opportunities and resources for dramatic play, creating a supportive environment, and participating in these activities with children, parents and caregivers can foster a love for role-playing and drama and lifelong learning. Through the rich and dynamic experiences of role-playing and drama, children can develop essential skills, build confidence, and experience the profound benefits of creative expression and social interaction.

 papa

"Music and movement activities promote physical and emotional growth. They provide an outlet for self-expression and joy. Engaging with music and movement helps children develop coordination and rhythm."

♥♥♥

ELEVEN

FOSTERING A GROWTH MINDSET

Fostering a growth mindset in children is fundamental to their development and success in various aspects of life. A growth mindset, as defined by psychologist Carol Dweck, is the belief that abilities and intelligence can be developed through effort, perseverance, and learning. In contrast, a fixed mindset is the belief that abilities and intelligence are static and unchangeable traits. Encouraging a growth mindset in children involves helping them understand that their abilities can grow with time and effort, which can profoundly impact their motivation, resilience, and overall approach to challenges.

One of the first steps in fostering a growth mindset is to teach children about the concept itself. Helping them understand the difference between a fixed mindset and a growth mindset can empower them to recognize and challenge their own limiting beliefs. This can be done through age-appropriate discussions, books, and stories that illustrate the principles of growth and the power of perseverance. For example, sharing stories of famous individuals who overcame significant obstacles through hard work and determination can inspire children to adopt a growth mindset.

Language plays a crucial role in shaping children's beliefs about their abilities. Using growth-oriented language and praise can encourage children to embrace challenges and view effort as a pathway to improvement. Instead of praising children solely for their innate talents or intelligence, it is more effective to praise their effort, strategies, and persistence. For example, saying "You worked really hard on this project and it shows!" or "I'm proud of how you kept trying different ways to solve that problem" focuses on the process rather than the outcome. This type of praise reinforces the idea that effort and perseverance lead to growth and success.

Modeling a growth mindset is another important way to foster it in children. Parents, caregivers, and educators can demonstrate a growth mindset through their own attitudes and behaviors. Sharing personal experiences of overcoming challenges, learning from mistakes, and persevering through difficulties can provide powerful examples for children. By openly discussing their own learning processes and the value of effort, adults can show children that growth and improvement are possible for everyone. Additionally, adults can model a positive attitude towards mistakes and failures, emphasizing that they are natural parts of the learning process and opportunities for growth.

Creating an environment that supports a growth mindset involves providing opportunities for children to take on challenges and learn from their experiences. Encouraging children to set goals, take risks, and try new things can help them develop a sense of agency and confidence in their ability to grow. It's important to create a safe and supportive atmosphere where children feel comfortable taking risks and making mistakes without fear of judgment. This can involve setting clear expectations, providing constructive feedback, and offering guidance and support as children navigate challenges.

Teaching children specific strategies for learning and problem-solving can also promote a growth mindset. For example, teaching them how to break down complex tasks into smaller, manageable steps can make challenges feel less overwhelming. Encouraging children to use self-talk and positive affirmations can help them stay motivated and focused on their goals. Additionally, teaching children how to seek out and use resources, such as books, online tutorials, or help from others, can empower them to take charge of their own learning and growth.

Encouraging children to reflect on their learning experiences and progress is another effective way to foster a growth mindset. Regular reflection helps children recognize their growth, understand the strategies that work for them, and identify areas for further improvement. This can be done through activities such as journaling, discussions, or creating visual representations of their learning journey, such as progress charts or goal-setting boards. Reflection also helps children develop a deeper understanding of their own learning processes and reinforces the idea that growth is a continuous journey.

In addition to individual efforts, fostering a growth mindset involves creating a culture of growth and learning within the family, school, or community. This can be achieved by celebrating effort and progress, sharing success stories, and encouraging a collaborative approach to learning and problem-solving. In a growth-oriented culture, individuals support and inspire each other to strive for improvement and embrace challenges. This type of environment fosters a sense of belonging and collective growth, where everyone is committed to learning and development.

One of the challenges in fostering a growth mindset is addressing and transforming existing fixed mindset beliefs. Children may have internalized fixed mindset messages from various sources, such as previous experiences, societal expectations, or cultural influences. It's important to recognize and challenge these beliefs by providing evidence of growth and change. For example, sharing examples of personal growth, highlighting improvements over time, and discussing the malleability of the brain can help children understand that their abilities are not fixed and can be developed through effort and practice.

Encouraging a love for learning is also central to fostering a growth mindset. When children are motivated by curiosity and a desire to learn, they are more likely to embrace challenges and persist in the face of difficulties. Providing opportunities for exploration, discovery, and hands-on learning can ignite children's passion for learning. This can involve engaging in activities that align with their interests, such as science experiments, creative projects, or outdoor adventures. By fostering a love for learning, children develop intrinsic motivation and a lifelong commitment to growth and self-improvement.

Collaboration and peer support play a significant role in fostering a growth mindset. Working with others on projects, problem-solving tasks, or group activities allows children to learn from each other, share different perspectives, and develop a sense of community. Encouraging collaborative learning experiences, such as group discussions, team sports, or cooperative games, can help children understand the value of collective effort and mutual support. Peer feedback and encouragement can also reinforce growth mindset principles and inspire children to strive for improvement.

Another important aspect of fostering a growth mindset is helping children develop resilience and coping skills. Resilience involves the ability to bounce back from setbacks and persevere through challenges. Teaching children coping strategies, such as deep breathing, positive self-talk, and problem-solving techniques, can help them manage stress and stay focused on their goals. Encouraging children to view setbacks as temporary and learning opportunities can build their resilience and determination. By developing resilience, children are better equipped to handle challenges and setbacks with a positive and growth-oriented mindset.

Incorporating mindfulness practices into daily routines can also support the development of a growth mindset. Mindfulness involves being present in the moment and paying attention to one's thoughts, feelings, and experiences without judgment. Mindfulness practices, such as meditation, deep breathing exercises, or mindful movement, can help children develop self-awareness and emotional regulation. These practices can also promote a sense of calm and focus, making it easier for children to approach challenges with a clear and open mind. By incorporating mindfulness into their daily lives, children can develop the mental and emotional skills needed to cultivate a growth mindset.

Recognizing and addressing the impact of praise and feedback on children's mindset is crucial. While praise can be motivating, it's important to ensure that it is focused on effort and process rather than fixed traits. For example, praising a child for their hard work, persistence, and strategies encourages a growth mindset, while praising them solely for their intelligence or talent can reinforce a fixed mindset. Providing specific and constructive feedback that highlights areas for improvement and offers guidance on how to achieve growth can help children develop a sense of agency and control over their learning.

Parents, caregivers, and educators can also support the development of a growth mindset by modeling lifelong learning and continuous improvement. Demonstrating a commitment to learning new skills, pursuing personal goals, and embracing challenges can inspire children to adopt similar attitudes. Sharing experiences of learning, growth, and overcoming obstacles can provide valuable lessons and motivation for children. By embodying a growth mindset, adults can create a positive and supportive environment that encourages children to strive for excellence and believe in their potential.

Fostering a growth mindset in children is essential for their development and success in various aspects of life. By teaching children about the principles of a growth mindset, using growth-oriented language, modeling positive attitudes, creating supportive environments, and providing opportunities for exploration and learning, parents, caregivers, and educators can help children develop the skills and attitudes needed to embrace challenges and persevere through difficulties. Encouraging reflection, collaboration, resilience, mindfulness, and a love for learning further supports the development of a growth mindset. Through these efforts, children can develop the confidence, motivation, and determination to reach their full potential and achieve their goals.

"Art and craft activities offer endless opportunities for creative exploration. They encourage children to experiment with different materials and techniques. These activities also promote problem-solving and critical thinking."

▷▷▷

TWELVE

TECHNOLOGY AND DIGITAL CREATIVITY

Technology and digital creativity are integral to contemporary childhood development, offering numerous benefits that extend beyond mere entertainment. The digital world provides children with a vast array of tools and platforms that can enhance their creativity, foster cognitive growth, and prepare them for a future where technological literacy is essential. Embracing technology and digital creativity involves understanding the balance between screen time and other activities, ensuring that children use technology in ways that are enriching and educational.

One of the most significant advantages of technology in fostering digital creativity is the access it provides to a wide range of creative tools. Software for drawing, painting, music composition, video editing, and animation offers children the ability to express their ideas in diverse and dynamic ways. These tools often come with features that traditional methods cannot provide, such as unlimited undo functions, extensive color palettes, and advanced editing capabilities. For instance, digital drawing tablets allow children to experiment with various styles and techniques without the constraints of physical materials. This flexibility encourages experimentation and innovation, essential components of the creative process.

Digital creativity also extends to programming and coding, which are becoming increasingly important skills in the modern world. Learning to code encourages logical thinking, problem-solving, and creativity. Platforms like Scratch, Tynker, and Code.org offer child-friendly interfaces where children can create their own games, stories, and animations through coding. These platforms make learning to code fun and accessible, transforming abstract concepts into tangible projects. By engaging in coding activities, children develop an understanding of how technology works and learn to create with it, rather than just consuming it.

Moreover, technology facilitates collaborative creativity, allowing children to work together on projects regardless of geographical boundaries. Online platforms and tools such as Google Docs, collaborative whiteboards, and project management software enable children to share ideas, provide feedback, and co-create in real time. This collaboration mirrors the increasingly interconnected nature of the modern workplace and teaches children valuable skills in teamwork, communication, and project management. For example, children can work together to produce a digital magazine, create a collaborative piece of art, or develop a joint coding project, learning to leverage each other's strengths and perspectives.

The internet provides access to a vast repository of resources and inspiration. Websites like YouTube, Khan Academy, and Coursera offer tutorials and courses on almost any topic imaginable. Children can learn new skills, explore different art forms, and draw inspiration from the work of others. This access to a global knowledge base allows children to pursue their interests deeply and broadly, often far beyond what traditional educational resources can provide. For instance, a child interested in animation can find step-by-step tutorials from professional animators, participate in online communities, and showcase their work to a global audience.

While the benefits of technology and digital creativity are substantial, it is essential to manage screen time to ensure that children engage with technology in healthy and productive ways. Excessive screen time can lead to physical issues such as eye strain and poor posture, as well as negatively impact social skills and physical activity. Parents and caregivers play a crucial role in setting boundaries and encouraging a balanced approach to technology use. This involves setting time limits, encouraging breaks, and promoting a mix of digital and offline activities. It's also important to foster an understanding of when and how to use technology responsibly.

Creating a supportive environment for digital creativity includes providing access to appropriate tools and resources. Ensuring that children have access to reliable devices, internet connectivity, and age-appropriate software and applications is crucial. Additionally, guiding children in choosing educational and creative apps over purely recreational ones can make their screen time more productive. Parents and caregivers can explore these tools together with their children, learning about the functionalities and possibilities, and setting up projects that integrate digital creativity with learning goals.

Encouraging children to take part in digital storytelling is another powerful way to harness technology for creative expression. Digital storytelling involves using multimedia elements such as text, images, audio, and video to tell stories. Platforms like Storybird, Adobe Spark, and WeVideo provide children with the tools to create and share their stories digitally. This form of storytelling allows children to combine their creative writing skills with technical skills, enhancing their ability to communicate complex ideas and narratives. By creating digital stories, children learn to think critically about how to convey their messages effectively through different media.

Virtual reality (VR) and augmented reality (AR) are emerging technologies that offer new dimensions for digital creativity. These technologies allow children to create and interact with three-dimensional environments and experiences. For example, VR can be used to build virtual worlds where children can explore and manipulate objects, while AR can overlay digital information onto the real world, creating interactive learning experiences. Applications like Tilt Brush and CoSpaces Edu enable children to create VR art and AR experiences, blending the physical and digital worlds in innovative ways. These immersive technologies stimulate imagination and provide unique opportunities for creative exploration and learning.

Incorporating digital creativity into education can enhance traditional learning methods. Interactive digital tools can make subjects like math, science, and history more engaging and accessible. For instance, educational software and apps can turn complex mathematical concepts into interactive games, making learning fun and intuitive. Science simulations can allow children to conduct virtual experiments that would be difficult or impossible to perform in a traditional classroom. Historical events can be brought to life through interactive timelines and digital recreations, making history more vivid and relatable. By integrating digital creativity into the curriculum, educators can provide a more engaging and effective learning experience.

It is also essential to teach children about digital citizenship and ethical use of technology. As children create and share digital content, they need to understand the importance of respecting intellectual property, maintaining privacy, and being responsible digital citizens. Educating children about cyberbullying, online safety, and the ethical implications of their digital activities helps them navigate the digital world responsibly. Encouraging discussions about these topics and setting clear guidelines for online behavior can help children develop a strong sense of digital ethics.

Parents and caregivers can further support digital creativity by participating in projects and activities with their children. Co-creating digital content, such as making a family video, designing a digital scrapbook, or building a website together, can be a bonding experience that also enhances children's technical skills. Engaging in these activities together allows parents to guide their children in using technology creatively and responsibly. It also provides an opportunity to discuss the content they create and consume, fostering critical thinking about media and technology.

Recognizing and celebrating children's digital creations is crucial for encouraging continued exploration and creativity. Sharing their work with family, friends, and online communities can boost their confidence and motivation. Platforms like YouTube, social media, and digital portfolios provide venues for children to showcase their projects and receive feedback. Positive reinforcement and constructive feedback from parents, teachers, and peers can help children refine their skills and develop a sense of pride in their accomplishments.

Finally, it is important to stay informed about the latest technological trends and tools that can support digital creativity. The rapid pace of technological advancement means that new tools and platforms are constantly emerging, offering new possibilities for creative expression. Parents, educators, and caregivers can benefit from staying up-to-date with these developments and exploring how they can be integrated into children's activities and learning experiences. Attending workshops, participating in online courses, and joining professional communities can provide valuable insights and resources for fostering digital creativity.

Technology and digital creativity play a vital role in contemporary childhood development, offering numerous benefits that extend across cognitive, emotional, social, and technical domains. By providing access to creative tools, encouraging collaborative projects, integrating digital creativity into education, and promoting responsible use of technology, parents, caregivers, and educators can help children harness the full potential of the digital world. Balancing screen time with other activities, staying informed about technological advancements, and celebrating children's digital creations further support their growth and development. Through the dynamic and enriching experiences of digital creativity, children can develop essential skills, explore their passions, and prepare for a future where technological literacy is increasingly important.

"Imaginative play and role-playing are
fundamental to social and emotional development.
They allow children to explore different perspectives
and build empathy. These activities also enhance
communication skills."

ꕥꕥꕥ

THIRTEEN

COLLABORATION AND TEAMWORK

Collaboration and teamwork are fundamental skills that children must develop to navigate the complexities of the modern world. These skills are essential not only for academic success but also for personal and professional growth. Learning to work effectively with others enables children to share ideas, solve problems, and achieve common goals. It also fosters empathy, communication, and social interaction, which are crucial for building strong relationships and thriving in diverse environments.

One of the most significant benefits of collaboration and teamwork is the enhancement of communication skills. When children work together on a project, they must express their ideas clearly, listen to others, and engage in meaningful dialogue. This exchange of ideas helps children develop their verbal and non-verbal communication skills. They learn to articulate their thoughts, ask questions, and provide constructive feedback. These interactions also teach children the importance of active listening, as they must understand and consider the perspectives of their teammates. Effective communication is a cornerstone of successful teamwork, and developing these skills early on sets the foundation for future collaboration.

Collaboration and teamwork also promote problem-solving and critical thinking. When children work together, they are often faced with challenges that require collective brainstorming and decision-making. This process encourages them to think creatively and critically, as they must evaluate different solutions and choose the best course of action. Working in teams allows children to leverage diverse viewpoints and expertise, leading to more innovative and effective problem-solving. For example, a group of students working on a science project might each bring unique strengths and knowledge to the table, resulting in a more comprehensive and well-rounded solution than any individual could achieve alone. These collaborative experiences help children develop the cognitive flexibility and resilience needed to tackle complex problems.

Emotional growth is another crucial aspect of collaboration and teamwork. Working with others can be a powerful way for children to develop empathy and emotional intelligence. By interacting with peers in collaborative settings, children learn to recognize and respond to the emotions and needs of others. They become more attuned to the dynamics of group interactions and develop a greater understanding of how their actions and words affect their teammates. This emotional awareness fosters a sense of compassion and respect, which are essential for building strong and supportive relationships. Additionally, collaboration and teamwork provide opportunities for children to develop their self-regulation skills, as they must manage their emotions and behavior to work effectively with others.

Socially, collaboration and teamwork teach children important interpersonal skills. Participating in group activities requires children to navigate social dynamics, such as negotiating roles, resolving conflicts, and building consensus. These experiences help children develop their social competence and adaptability, as they learn to work with diverse individuals and personalities.

Collaborative activities also provide a sense of belonging and community, as children work towards common goals and celebrate their achievements together. This sense of camaraderie and shared purpose can boost children's self-esteem and confidence, as they feel valued and supported by their peers.

For parents and educators, fostering collaboration and teamwork involves creating opportunities for children to work together in meaningful ways. This can be done by incorporating group projects, cooperative games, and collaborative learning activities into daily routines and curricula. Providing a variety of collaborative experiences, such as academic projects, sports teams, and creative endeavors, allows children to develop their teamwork skills in different contexts and discover their strengths and interests.

Creating a supportive environment for collaboration and teamwork also involves setting clear expectations and providing guidance and feedback. It is important to establish norms and rules for group interactions, such as taking turns, listening actively, and respecting others' opinions. Providing structured activities and frameworks, such as roles and responsibilities, can help children understand how to work together effectively. Additionally, offering regular feedback and encouragement can help children reflect on their teamwork experiences and identify areas for improvement.

One effective way to promote collaboration and teamwork is through project-based learning. Project-based learning involves students working together to explore real-world problems and create meaningful solutions. This approach encourages active engagement, critical thinking, and collaboration, as students must research, plan, and execute their projects collectively. For example, a project-based learning activity might involve students working together to design and build a sustainable garden for their school. This project would require them to collaborate on tasks such as researching plants, planning the garden layout, and constructing the garden beds. Through this process, students develop their teamwork skills and gain a deeper understanding of the subject matter.

Sports and physical activities also provide valuable opportunities for collaboration and teamwork. Participating in team sports teaches children the importance of cooperation, communication, and trust. They learn to work together towards a common goal, support their teammates, and celebrate their successes and failures as a team. These experiences help children develop a sense of discipline, responsibility, and sportsmanship. Additionally, team sports provide a fun and engaging way for children to build their physical fitness and develop a lifelong appreciation for physical activity.

Creative endeavors, such as music, drama, and art, offer another avenue for fostering collaboration and teamwork. Participating in a school play, joining a choir, or working on a group art project requires children to collaborate and coordinate their efforts to achieve a common goal. These activities encourage children to express themselves creatively while also learning to appreciate and support the creative contributions of others. Collaborative creative projects can also enhance children's cultural awareness and appreciation, as they explore diverse artistic traditions and perspectives.

Technology can also play a role in promoting collaboration and teamwork. Digital tools and platforms, such as collaborative writing software, online discussion forums, and virtual project management tools, enable children to work together on projects regardless of physical location. These tools facilitate communication, organization, and collaboration, making it easier for children to share ideas, track progress, and manage tasks. For example, students working on a group presentation can use collaborative writing software to draft and edit their slides together in real time, even if they are not in the same room. Technology can also provide opportunities for global collaboration, as children connect with peers from different countries and cultures to work on shared projects.

Parents and educators can further support collaboration and teamwork by modeling these skills in their own interactions. Demonstrating effective communication, cooperation, and conflict resolution in everyday situations provides children with positive examples to emulate. Additionally, involving children in family or classroom decisions and projects can give them practical experience in working together and contributing to a common goal. For example, planning a family vacation or organizing a classroom event can be an opportunity for children to practice their teamwork skills and take on responsibilities.

Encouraging reflection and self-assessment is also important for developing collaboration and teamwork skills. Providing opportunities for children to reflect on their group experiences, identify what went well, and discuss areas for improvement can help them develop a deeper understanding of effective teamwork. Reflection activities, such as group discussions, peer feedback, and self-assessment checklists, can promote self-awareness and continuous growth. For example, after completing a group project, students can discuss what strategies worked best, how they resolved conflicts, and what they could do differently in future collaborations.

Celebrating and recognizing teamwork achievements is crucial for reinforcing the value of collaboration. Acknowledging the efforts and contributions of all team members fosters a sense of pride and motivation. This can be done through awards, certificates, or public recognition, such as presenting projects at school assemblies or sharing successes with the broader community. Celebrating teamwork achievements not only boosts children's confidence but also reinforces the importance of working together towards common goals.

Collaboration and teamwork are essential skills that children must develop to navigate the complexities of the modern world. These skills enhance communication, problem-solving, emotional growth, and social competence, providing a strong foundation for academic and personal success. By creating opportunities for meaningful collaboration, providing guidance and feedback, and modeling effective teamwork, parents and educators can help children develop these critical skills. Through the diverse experiences of working together, children learn to appreciate the value of cooperation, empathy, and shared goals, preparing them for a future where collaboration and teamwork are increasingly important.

ᗡᗡᗡ

"Building and construction play develops spatial
awareness and fine motor skills. It encourages
children to think critically and solve problems.
These activities foster creativity and innovation."

ᘖᘖᘖ

FOURTEEN

CREATIVE COOKING AND BAKING

Creative cooking and baking are wonderful activities that offer numerous benefits for children's development, encompassing physical, cognitive, emotional, and social growth. Engaging children in the kitchen not only teaches them valuable life skills but also provides opportunities for creativity, experimentation, and learning. Through cooking and baking, children can explore new flavors and textures, develop fine motor skills, practice math and science concepts, and enjoy the process of creating something unique and delicious.

One of the most immediate benefits of cooking and baking is the development of fine motor skills. Activities such as chopping vegetables, measuring ingredients, kneading dough, and stirring mixtures require precise movements and coordination. These actions help strengthen the small muscles in the hands and fingers, which are crucial for tasks such as writing, drawing, and using tools. For younger children, tasks like pouring liquids, rolling dough, and decorating cookies can be particularly effective in enhancing their dexterity and control. By regularly engaging in cooking and baking activities, children develop the fine motor skills necessary for success in both academic and everyday tasks.

Cooking and baking also offer rich opportunities for cognitive development. The kitchen is a practical setting where children can apply and reinforce math and science concepts. Measuring ingredients requires an understanding of quantities, fractions, and units of measurement. Following a recipe involves reading comprehension, sequencing, and following instructions. Baking, in particular, is a science that involves chemical reactions, such as the role of yeast in bread rising or the effects of heat on ingredients. By engaging in these activities, children learn to observe, hypothesize, and experiment, enhancing their problem-solving and critical thinking skills. For example, they might learn about the importance of accurate measurements when they see the difference between a perfectly risen cake and one that has collapsed due to incorrect proportions.

Emotionally, creative cooking and baking provide valuable opportunities for self-expression and emotional exploration. Creating a dish or baked good allows children to bring their ideas and imagination to life, providing a sense of accomplishment and pride. This process of creation and expression can boost children's self-esteem and confidence. Additionally, cooking and baking offer opportunities for children to set and achieve goals, which can foster a sense of purpose and motivation. The focus and concentration required for these activities can also provide a calming and therapeutic effect, helping children to manage stress and anxiety. For instance, the repetitive motion of kneading dough or the soothing rhythm of stirring a pot can be very grounding and meditative.

Socially, cooking and baking sprvide opportunities for interaction and collaboration. Preparing a meal or baking a batch of cookies can be a shared experience that brings family and friends together. Working in the kitchen requires communication, cooperation, and coordination, as children must share tasks, take turns, and work towards a common goal. These interactions help children develop important social skills such as empathy, cooperation, and conflict resolution. Additionally, cooking and baking together provide a sense of belonging and community, as children contribute to family traditions and create shared memories. For example, making holiday cookies or preparing a special meal for a family celebration can strengthen bonds and create lasting traditions.

For parents and caregivers, involving children in cooking and baking activities involves creating a supportive and safe environment. Ensuring that the kitchen is child-friendly and that children are supervised and guided during these activities is crucial for safety. Providing age-appropriate tasks and tools, such as child-sized utensils and step stools, allows children to participate more fully and confidently. Encouraging children to take on responsibilities, such as setting the table, washing fruits and vegetables, or stirring ingredients, helps them develop a sense of independence and capability.

Encouraging creativity in cooking and baking involves allowing children to experiment with flavors, ingredients, and presentation. Providing a variety of ingredients and encouraging children to create their own recipes or variations can stimulate their imagination and curiosity. For example, children might enjoy creating their own pizza toppings, designing unique sandwich combinations, or inventing new cookie recipes. These activities encourage children to think creatively and develop their culinary skills. Additionally, involving children in the planning and decision-making process, such as choosing recipes, making shopping lists, and selecting ingredients, helps them develop a sense of ownership and pride in their culinary creations.

Cooking and baking also offer opportunities for cultural exploration and appreciation. Exploring recipes from different cultures introduces children to diverse flavors, ingredients, and cooking techniques. This exposure helps broaden their culinary horizons and fosters an appreciation for cultural diversity. Preparing dishes from various cultures can be a fun and educational way to learn about different traditions and customs. For example, making sushi, baking challah, or preparing a traditional Indian curry can provide insights into Japanese, Jewish, and Indian cultures, respectively. These activities can also prompt discussions about geography, history, and cultural practices, enriching children's understanding of the world.

Technology can play a role in enhancing creative cooking and baking experiences. Digital tools such as cooking apps, online tutorials, and virtual cooking classes offer new and exciting ways for children to learn and explore culinary arts. These resources provide access to a wealth of recipes, instructional videos, and interactive cooking activities that can inspire and guide children in their culinary adventures. For example, using a tablet to follow a step-by-step video tutorial on making macarons or accessing an app that generates random recipe ideas can make cooking and baking more engaging and accessible. However, it's important to balance screen time with hands-on, real-world cooking experiences to ensure a well-rounded culinary education.

Parents and caregivers can further support creative cooking and baking by participating in these activities with their children. Cooking and baking together can create joyful and meaningful shared experiences and strengthen the parent-child bond. By working alongside their children, parents can model culinary skills, introduce new techniques, and provide guidance and support. Asking open-ended questions about children's culinary creations, offering positive feedback, and showing genuine interest in their creative process can make a significant impact on a child's confidence and motivation. For example, praising a child's effort in decorating a cake or discussing the flavors they chose for a salad can encourage them to continue exploring their culinary interests.

Incorporating cooking and baking into everyday activities can further enhance children's engagement and enjoyment. Simple tasks such as preparing breakfast, packing lunches, or making snacks can be opportunities for children to practice their culinary skills and contribute to family routines. These activities do not need to be time-consuming or complex; even a few minutes of involvement in the kitchen can have a positive impact. Additionally, finding inspiration from everyday experiences, such as using seasonal fruits and vegetables, creating dishes inspired by favorite books or movies, or preparing meals for special occasions, can provide fresh ideas for culinary creativity.

Encouraging children to reflect on their cooking and baking experiences can help them develop a deeper understanding and appreciation of the culinary arts. Providing opportunities for children to evaluate their creations, identify what went well, and discuss areas for improvement can promote self-awareness and continuous growth. Reflection activities, such as keeping a cooking journal, participating in family taste tests, or sharing their creations with others, can enhance children's culinary skills and confidence. For example, asking children to write about their favorite recipe, what they learned from making it, and how they might improve it next time can deepen their understanding and enjoyment of cooking and baking.

Celebrating and recognizing children's culinary efforts is crucial for fostering a love for cooking and baking. Acknowledging their creativity, effort, and achievements reinforces the value of these activities and encourages them to continue exploring their culinary passions. Creating opportunities for children to showcase their culinary creations, such as hosting family cook-offs, organizing baking contests, or preparing meals for special occasions, can boost their confidence and motivation. These events also provide a platform for children to receive feedback and appreciation from others, further enhancing their self-esteem and sense of accomplishment.

Creative cooking and baking are essential activities that offer a multitude of benefits for children's development. These activities enhance fine motor skills, cognitive growth, emotional well-being, and social interaction. By providing a supportive and safe environment, encouraging creativity and experimentation, and participating in these activities with children, parents and caregivers can foster a love for cooking and baking and lifelong learning. Through the rich and dynamic experiences of creative cooking and baking, children can develop essential skills, build confidence, and experience the profound benefits of culinary expression and exploration.

❧❧❧

"Supporting a growth mindset teaches children that abilities can be developed through effort and learning. It encourages them to embrace challenges and persist in the face of setbacks. This mindset is crucial for lifelong success."

♡♡♡

FIFTEEN

EXPLORING DIFFERENT CULTURES

Exploring different cultures is an enriching and essential part of childhood development. Exposure to diverse cultures enhances children's understanding of the world, fosters empathy, and promotes open-mindedness. By learning about different traditions, languages, cuisines, and histories, children develop a broader perspective and a deeper appreciation for cultural diversity. This exploration helps build a foundation for respectful and harmonious relationships in an increasingly interconnected global society.

One of the most significant benefits of exploring different cultures is the development of cultural awareness and sensitivity. When children learn about the customs, beliefs, and practices of various cultures, they begin to appreciate the richness and complexity of human societies. This awareness helps children understand that their way of life is just one of many, fostering a sense of curiosity and respect for different perspectives. For example, learning about festivals such as Diwali, Chinese New Year, or Hanukkah can introduce children to the diverse ways in which people celebrate important events and milestones. This knowledge helps children see the value in traditions that differ from their own and encourages them to approach cultural differences with an open mind.

Exploring different cultures also promotes empathy and emotional intelligence. When children hear stories, watch films, or read books about people from different cultural backgrounds, they are given the opportunity to put themselves in others' shoes. This practice of perspective-taking helps children develop empathy, as they learn to understand and share the feelings of others. For instance, reading a story about a child growing up in a different country can help children appreciate the challenges and joys that come with living in a different cultural context. This empathetic understanding is crucial for building inclusive and supportive communities, where individuals from diverse backgrounds feel valued and respected.

Cognitive development is another important benefit of exploring different cultures. Exposure to diverse cultural practices and ways of thinking stimulates children's cognitive growth by challenging them to consider new and varied perspectives. This exposure can enhance critical thinking and problem-solving skills, as children learn to navigate and appreciate complexity. For example, studying the architectural styles of different cultures, such as the intricate designs of Islamic architecture or the minimalist aesthetics of Japanese architecture, can inspire children to think creatively and appreciate different forms of artistic expression. Engaging with diverse cultural content encourages children to question assumptions, make connections, and develop a more nuanced understanding of the world.

Language learning is an integral part of exploring different cultures and offers significant cognitive and social benefits. Learning a new language opens up a world of opportunities for children, allowing them to communicate with people from different cultural backgrounds and access a wealth of knowledge and literature.

Bilingualism and multilingualism have been shown to improve cognitive flexibility, memory, and problem-solving skills. For instance, children who learn to speak Spanish can connect with Spanish-speaking communities, read Spanish literature, and understand the cultural nuances embedded in the language. Language learning also promotes cultural empathy, as it encourages children to appreciate the intricacies and beauty of different languages.

Food is another powerful way to explore different cultures. Trying new cuisines and learning about the culinary traditions of various cultures can be a delightful and educational experience for children. Cooking and tasting dishes from around the world helps children understand the significance of food in different cultures and the ways in which culinary practices are influenced by geography, history, and tradition. For example, preparing Italian pasta, Japanese sushi, or Ethiopian injera can introduce children to the ingredients, flavors, and cooking techniques unique to these cultures. Sharing meals from different cultures can also foster a sense of community and celebration, as food often brings people together in meaningful ways.

Art and music are universal forms of expression that provide rich opportunities for cultural exploration. Engaging with the visual and performing arts of different cultures helps children appreciate the diverse ways in which people express their creativity and identity. For instance, exploring the vibrant colors and patterns of African art, the intricate details of Indian classical dance, or the soulful rhythms of Latin American music can inspire children and broaden their artistic horizons. Participating in cultural art and music activities, such as attending performances, visiting museums, or creating art inspired by different cultural traditions, allows children to connect with and celebrate the beauty of cultural diversity.

Travel, whether physical or virtual, is another impactful way to explore different cultures. Visiting new places and experiencing different environments firsthand can leave lasting impressions on children. Traveling allows children to immerse themselves in new cultural contexts, observe daily life, and interact with people from diverse backgrounds. Even if physical travel is not possible, virtual tours and online resources can provide valuable cultural experiences. For example, virtual tours of world-famous landmarks, such as the Great Wall of China, the Pyramids of Egypt, or the Eiffel Tower, can spark children's curiosity and provide insights into the cultural and historical significance of these sites. Travel experiences, both real and virtual, help children develop a sense of global citizenship and a deeper appreciation for the diversity of the world.

Incorporating cultural exploration into education can significantly enhance the learning experience. Integrating multicultural content into the curriculum helps children see the relevance of cultural diversity in various subjects, such as history, literature, geography, and social studies. For example, studying the contributions of diverse cultures to scientific advancements, literature, and art can provide a more inclusive and comprehensive understanding of human achievement. Celebrating cultural heritage months, such as Black History Month, Hispanic Heritage Month, or Asian Pacific American Heritage Month, can provide opportunities for focused learning and appreciation of the contributions and experiences of different cultural groups.

Parents and caregivers play a crucial role in fostering cultural exploration and appreciation. Creating a culturally rich home environment, where diversity is celebrated and valued, can significantly impact children's attitudes towards different cultures. This can involve incorporating diverse books, music, and art into the home, celebrating cultural holidays and traditions, and encouraging open discussions about cultural differences and similarities. Parents can also model inclusive behavior and attitudes, demonstrating respect and curiosity towards different cultures. For example, attending cultural festivals, visiting cultural institutions, or participating in cultural exchange programs as a family can provide valuable learning experiences and foster a sense of appreciation for cultural diversity.

Community involvement is another important aspect of cultural exploration. Engaging with local cultural organizations, participating in community events, and building relationships with people from diverse backgrounds can provide meaningful cultural experiences for children. Volunteering with cultural organizations, attending cultural workshops, or participating in community dialogues can help children understand the importance of cultural diversity in building strong, inclusive communities. Community involvement also provides opportunities for children to develop their social and leadership skills, as they work with others to promote cultural understanding and appreciation.

Technology can also facilitate cultural exploration, providing access to a wealth of resources and experiences. Online platforms, educational websites, and social media offer numerous opportunities to learn about different cultures and connect with people from around the world. Virtual exchanges, online cultural festivals, and interactive learning modules can provide immersive and engaging cultural experiences. For example, participating in a virtual pen pal program can allow children to communicate with peers from different countries, exchange cultural insights, and develop cross-cultural friendships. Technology can also provide access to digital libraries, documentaries, and educational games that explore cultural topics, making cultural exploration more accessible and interactive.

Encouraging children to reflect on their cultural exploration experiences is crucial for deepening their understanding and appreciation of cultural diversity. Providing opportunities for children to discuss what they have learned, share their insights, and express their thoughts and feelings about different cultures can promote critical thinking and empathy. Reflection activities, such as journaling, group discussions, or creative projects, can help children process their experiences and develop a more nuanced understanding of cultural diversity. For example, creating a cultural scrapbook, writing reflections on cultural experiences, or presenting a cultural research project can provide meaningful ways for children to engage with and celebrate cultural diversity.

Recognizing and celebrating children's efforts in exploring different cultures is important for reinforcing the value of cultural diversity. Acknowledging their curiosity, effort, and achievements in learning about different cultures can boost their confidence and motivation. Creating opportunities for children to showcase their cultural knowledge and experiences, such as cultural fairs, presentations, or performances, can provide a platform for them to share their learning with others and receive positive feedback. Celebrating cultural exploration achievements also fosters a sense of pride and appreciation for cultural diversity, encouraging children to continue their cultural learning journey.

Exploring different cultures is an enriching and essential part of childhood development. Exposure to diverse cultures enhances children's understanding of the world, fosters empathy, and promotes open-mindedness. By learning about different traditions, languages, cuisines, and histories, children develop a broader perspective and a deeper appreciation for cultural diversity. Parents, educators, and caregivers can support cultural exploration by creating culturally rich environments, incorporating multicultural content into education, engaging with communities, leveraging technology, and encouraging reflection and celebration of cultural achievements. Through the rich and dynamic experiences of exploring different cultures, children can develop essential skills, build empathy and respect, and become informed and compassionate global citizens.

❥❥❥

"Technology and digital creativity open up new possibilities for expression and learning. They provide tools for innovation and collaboration. Balancing digital activities with real-world experiences enriches children's development."

❤❤❤

SIXTEEN

BALANCING STRUCTURE AND FREEDOM

Balancing structure and freedom is a fundamental aspect of raising and educating children. This delicate equilibrium is crucial for fostering independence, creativity, discipline, and resilience. Structure provides children with a sense of security and predictability, helping them understand expectations and boundaries. Freedom, on the other hand, encourages exploration, self-expression, and personal growth. Striking the right balance between these two elements can significantly impact a child's overall development and well-being.

Structure in a child's life typically comes in the form of routines, rules, and guidelines. These elements help create a stable environment where children can thrive. Routines, such as regular meal times, bedtimes, and study sessions, provide a sense of order and predictability. When children know what to expect, they feel more secure and are better able to manage their time and activities. For example, a consistent bedtime routine helps children get the rest they need, which is essential for their physical and cognitive development. Similarly, regular study sessions help children develop good study habits and time management skills, which are crucial for academic success.

Rules and guidelines play a crucial role in teaching children about acceptable behavior and boundaries. Clear and consistent rules help children understand what is expected of them and what behaviors are unacceptable. This understanding is essential for developing self-discipline and respect for others. For example, rules about screen time, homework, and chores teach children about responsibility and the importance of balancing different aspects of their lives. Enforcing these rules consistently helps children internalize them and develop a sense of accountability.

While structure is essential, it is equally important to provide children with freedom. Freedom allows children to explore their interests, make choices, and learn from their experiences. This autonomy is crucial for developing independence and self-confidence. When children are given the freedom to make decisions, they learn to take responsibility for their actions and develop problem-solving skills. For example, allowing children to choose their extracurricular activities or hobbies encourages them to pursue their passions and develop a sense of identity. This freedom to explore and experiment is essential for fostering creativity and innovation.

Balancing structure and freedom involves creating an environment where children feel secure and supported while also having the opportunity to explore and take risks. One way to achieve this balance is by providing a framework of structure within which children have the freedom to make choices. For example, parents can establish a routine for homework and chores but allow children to decide the order in which they complete their tasks. This approach provides the stability of structure while also giving children a sense of control over their activities.

Another important aspect of balancing structure and freedom is setting clear expectations and providing guidance while allowing children the space to learn from their experiences. For example, when setting rules about screen time, parents can explain the reasons behind the rules and involve children in discussions about healthy screen habits. This approach helps children understand the importance of balance and encourages them to develop self-regulation skills. Providing guidance and support while allowing children to make their own decisions fosters a sense of autonomy and responsibility.

Encouraging open communication is also essential for balancing structure and freedom. Creating an environment where children feel comfortable expressing their thoughts and feelings helps build trust and mutual respect. When children know that their opinions and preferences are valued, they are more likely to engage in discussions about rules and routines and feel a sense of ownership over their decisions. Open communication also allows parents to provide support and guidance when needed, helping children navigate challenges and learn from their experiences.

Flexibility is another key component of balancing structure and freedom. While routines and rules are important, it is also essential to be flexible and adapt to changing circumstances and needs. For example, during times of stress or transition, such as starting a new school or dealing with a family crisis, it may be necessary to adjust routines and expectations to provide additional support and stability. Being flexible and responsive to children's needs helps create a supportive environment where they feel understood and valued.

Encouraging independence and self-directed learning is also crucial for balancing structure and freedom. Providing opportunities for children to take initiative and pursue their interests helps them develop a sense of autonomy and confidence. For example, allowing children to set their own goals and create their own projects encourages them to take ownership of their learning and develop important life skills. This approach helps children develop a growth mindset, where they see challenges as opportunities for growth and learning.

Incorporating play and creative activities into daily routines is another important aspect of balancing structure and freedom. Play is essential for children's cognitive, social, and emotional development. Providing time and space for unstructured play allows children to explore their imagination, develop social skills, and manage stress. For example, allowing children to play freely with their peers or engage in creative activities such as drawing, building, or role-playing encourages them to express themselves and develop their creativity. Balancing structured activities with time for free play helps children develop a well-rounded set of skills and interests.

Setting realistic and achievable goals is also important for balancing structure and freedom. Helping children set goals that are challenging but attainable provides them with a sense of direction and purpose. It also teaches them the value of perseverance and hard work. For example, setting a goal to improve a skill or complete a project provides children with a sense of accomplishment and boosts their self-esteem. Providing support and encouragement along the way helps children stay motivated and focused on their goals.

Recognizing and celebrating children's achievements is crucial for reinforcing the balance between structure and freedom. Acknowledging their efforts and successes helps build their confidence and encourages them to continue striving for their goals. Celebrating achievements also helps children develop a positive attitude towards challenges and setbacks, seeing them as opportunities for growth and learning. For example, celebrating a child's progress in learning a new skill or completing a challenging project helps them feel valued and supported.

Balancing structure and freedom also involves providing opportunities for children to develop their social and emotional skills. Encouraging children to build relationships and engage in social activities helps them develop empathy, communication, and teamwork skills. For example, participating in group activities, such as sports, clubs, or community service, helps children learn to work with others and develop a sense of belonging. Providing opportunities for children to develop their social and emotional skills helps them build strong and supportive relationships and navigate social challenges.

Creating a supportive and nurturing environment is essential for balancing structure and freedom. Providing children with a safe and loving home environment helps them feel secure and supported. This support provides a strong foundation for them to explore their interests and take risks. For example, providing a safe space for children to express their thoughts and feelings, offering guidance and support when needed, and encouraging them to pursue their passions helps them develop a sense of confidence and self-worth.

Balancing structure and freedom is a fundamental aspect of raising and educating children. Structure provides children with a sense of security and predictability, helping them understand expectations and boundaries. Freedom encourages exploration, self-expression, and personal growth, fostering independence and creativity. Striking the right balance between these two elements is crucial for children's overall development and well-being.

By providing a framework of structure within which children have the freedom to make choices, setting clear expectations and providing guidance, encouraging open communication and flexibility, promoting independence and self-directed learning, incorporating play and creative activities, setting realistic and achievable goals, recognizing and celebrating achievements, providing opportunities for social and emotional development, and creating a supportive and nurturing environment, parents and educators can help children thrive and reach their full potential. Through this balanced approach, children develop the skills, confidence, and resilience needed to navigate the complexities of life and achieve their goals.

❦❦❦

"Celebrating creative achievements highlights the
value of creativity in a child's life. It encourages
further exploration and engagement. Recognition
and praise boost their self-esteem and motivation."

ᐅᐅᐅ

SEVENTEEN

SUPPORTING INDIVIDUAL INTERESTS

Supporting individual interests in children is crucial for their overall development and well-being. When children pursue their passions and interests, they are more likely to develop a sense of purpose, intrinsic motivation, and a love for learning. Encouraging children to explore their unique interests helps them build self-confidence, develop specialized skills, and find joy in their activities. This approach to nurturing individual interests is essential for fostering creativity, resilience, and lifelong learning.

One of the first steps in supporting individual interests is recognizing and valuing each child's unique preferences and passions. Every child is different, with their own set of interests and talents. Some children may be drawn to sports, others to music, art, science, or literature. Understanding and appreciating these differences is crucial for providing the appropriate support and encouragement. Observing children's activities, listening to their conversations, and asking about their interests can provide valuable insights into what excites and motivates them. This awareness helps parents and educators create an environment where children's interests are recognized and nurtured.

Providing opportunities for exploration and discovery is essential for supporting individual interests. Children need the freedom to try out different activities and experiences to discover what they enjoy and where their talents lie. This exploration can involve a wide range of activities, such as joining clubs, taking classes, participating in community events, or simply experimenting with different hobbies at home. Encouraging children to explore various interests without pressure or expectations allows them to find their passions naturally. For example, a child interested in science might enjoy visiting a science museum, conducting simple experiments at home, or joining a science club. These experiences provide a platform for children to delve deeper into their interests and develop a genuine enthusiasm for learning.

Providing resources and support is another critical aspect of nurturing individual interests. Once a child's interests are identified, offering the necessary materials, tools, and resources can help them pursue their passions effectively. This support can include books, equipment, lessons, or access to facilities related to their interests. For instance, a child interested in painting might benefit from having a variety of art supplies, attending art classes, or visiting art galleries. Similarly, a child passionate about sports might need appropriate gear, coaching, and opportunities to participate in competitions. Ensuring that children have access to the resources they need to explore their interests fully helps them develop their skills and gain confidence in their abilities.

Encouragement and positive reinforcement play a vital role in supporting individual interests. Celebrating children's efforts and achievements, no matter how small, boosts their self-esteem and motivates them to continue pursuing their passions. Positive reinforcement can come in many forms, such as verbal praise, displaying their work, attending their performances or competitions, and providing constructive feedback. For example, praising a child's dedication to practicing a musical instrument or acknowledging their progress in a sport can make a significant impact on their confidence and motivation. This encouragement helps children feel valued and supported in their pursuits.

Balancing structured activities with free exploration is essential for fostering individual interests. While structured activities, such as classes or organized sports, provide valuable learning experiences and skill development, it is also important to allow time for unstructured, self-directed exploration. Free exploration enables children to experiment, take risks, and follow their curiosity without the constraints of formal instruction. For example, a child interested in writing might enjoy the freedom to create their own stories and poems outside of school assignments. Providing a balance between structured and unstructured activities ensures that children have the opportunity to develop their interests in a way that is both disciplined and creatively fulfilling.

Encouraging goal setting and self-reflection can enhance the pursuit of individual interests. Helping children set realistic and achievable goals related to their interests provides them with a sense of direction and purpose. These goals can be short-term, such as mastering a new skill, or long-term, such as completing a significant project or achieving a milestone in their chosen activity. Encouraging children to reflect on their progress and accomplishments helps them understand their growth and areas for improvement. This practice of setting goals and reflecting on their journey fosters a growth mindset, where children see challenges as opportunities for development and learning.

Involving children in decision-making processes related to their interests empowers them and fosters a sense of ownership. Allowing children to choose the activities they want to pursue, the goals they want to set, and the resources they need helps them develop decision-making skills and take responsibility for their learning. This involvement also reinforces their intrinsic motivation, as they are more likely to engage with activities they have chosen for themselves. For example, allowing a child interested in photography to decide on the subjects they want to capture or the techniques they want to learn encourages them to take initiative and explore their creativity.

Providing mentorship and guidance is another crucial aspect of supporting individual interests. Mentors, whether they are parents, teachers, coaches, or professionals in a particular field, can offer valuable insights, advice, and support. Mentorship helps children navigate the challenges and complexities of their chosen interests, providing them with the knowledge and skills they need to succeed. For example, a child interested in computer programming might benefit from having a mentor who can guide them through complex coding concepts and provide opportunities for real-world application. Mentors can also inspire and motivate children by sharing their own experiences and passion for the subject.

Creating a supportive and nurturing environment is essential for fostering individual interests. This environment should be free of judgment and pressure, allowing children to explore their interests at their own pace and in their own way. It is important to avoid comparing children to their peers or setting unrealistic expectations, as this can create stress and diminish their enjoyment of the activity. Instead, focus on each child's unique journey and celebrate their individual progress and achievements. Providing a safe and supportive space where children feel comfortable expressing their interests and pursuing their passions helps them develop a positive and confident self-image.

Encouraging collaboration and social interaction within the context of individual interests can enhance the learning experience.

Working with others who share similar interests provides opportunities for teamwork, communication, and mutual support. Collaborative activities, such as group projects, clubs, or workshops, allow children to learn from their peers, exchange ideas, and build a sense of community. For example, a child interested in drama might benefit from participating in a theater group where they can collaborate with others to create and perform plays. These social interactions help children develop important interpersonal skills and foster a sense of belonging.

Recognizing the role of failure and resilience in the pursuit of individual interests is crucial for long-term success. It is important to teach children that setbacks and failures are a natural part of the learning process and that they can learn valuable lessons from these experiences. Encouraging a growth mindset, where children view challenges as opportunities for growth, helps them develop resilience and perseverance. Providing support and encouragement during difficult times and helping children develop strategies for overcoming obstacles fosters a sense of determination and resilience. For example, if a child experiences a setback in a sports competition, guiding them to reflect on their performance, identify areas for improvement, and set new goals helps them build resilience and a positive attitude towards challenges.

Integrating individual interests into academic learning can enhance children's engagement and motivation in school. Connecting their passions with academic subjects makes learning more relevant and enjoyable. For example, a child interested in astronomy might find a deeper interest in physics and mathematics, or a child passionate about environmental conservation might engage more enthusiastically in science and geography lessons. Teachers can create interdisciplinary projects that allow students to explore their interests while meeting academic objectives. This integration helps children see the connections between their interests and academic learning, fostering a holistic and integrated approach to education.

Parents and educators can support individual interests by being lifelong learners themselves. Demonstrating a passion for learning and exploring new interests sets a positive example for children. When adults model curiosity and a love for learning, they inspire children to adopt a similar attitude towards their own interests. Engaging in learning activities together, such as reading, attending workshops, or exploring new hobbies, creates opportunities for shared experiences and mutual growth. This shared learning journey fosters a sense of connection and support, encouraging children to pursue their interests with enthusiasm and confidence.

In conclusion, supporting individual interests in children is essential for their overall development and well-being. By recognizing and valuing each child's unique preferences and passions, providing opportunities for exploration and discovery, offering resources and support, and encouraging goal setting and self-reflection, parents and educators can nurture children's interests and help them develop a love for learning. Creating a supportive and nurturing environment, involving children in decision-making processes, providing mentorship and guidance, and encouraging collaboration and social interaction further enhance the pursuit of individual interests.

Recognizing the role of failure and resilience, integrating interests into academic learning, and being lifelong learners themselves, adults can inspire and support children in their journey of exploration and growth. Through this holistic approach, children develop the skills, confidence, and intrinsic motivation needed to pursue their passions and achieve their full potential.

ppp

"Encouraging a child's curiosity is the key to
unlocking their potential. Questions drive learning
and innovation. A curious mind is a powerful tool
for discovery."

ᐅᐅᐅ

EIGHTEEN

THE POWER OF QUESTIONS

The power of questions in childhood development is immense and multifaceted. Questions stimulate curiosity, drive learning, and foster a deeper understanding of the world. For children, asking questions is a natural way to explore their environment, seek knowledge, and develop critical thinking skills. Encouraging a questioning mindset helps children become active learners, capable of independent thought and problem-solving. The ability to ask and answer questions effectively is a fundamental skill that shapes cognitive, social, and emotional development.

At the heart of the power of questions is the natural curiosity of children. From an early age, children are driven by a desire to understand their surroundings. Questions like "Why is the sky blue?" and "How do birds fly?" reflect their innate curiosity and eagerness to learn. This inquisitive nature is crucial for cognitive development, as it motivates children to seek out new information and experiences. When children ask questions, they engage in a process of inquiry that helps them make sense of the world. This process involves observation, hypothesis formation, experimentation, and reflection, all of which are key components of scientific thinking.

Encouraging children to ask questions and explore their curiosity is essential for fostering a love of learning. When adults respond positively to children's questions, they validate their curiosity and encourage further exploration. This positive reinforcement helps children develop confidence in their ability to seek and acquire knowledge. It also fosters a growth mindset, where children see learning as a continuous and enjoyable process. By providing answers, guiding research, and encouraging exploration, parents and educators can nurture a child's enthusiasm for learning and discovery.

Questions are powerful tools for developing critical thinking skills. When children ask questions, they learn to analyze information, evaluate evidence, and draw conclusions. This process helps them develop the ability to think critically and independently. For example, when a child asks, "What makes a plant grow?" they begin to explore concepts such as sunlight, water, and soil nutrients. Through this inquiry, they learn to gather information, compare different sources, and understand cause-and-effect relationships. Encouraging children to ask open-ended questions, which require more than a simple yes or no answer, promotes deeper thinking and reflection. Open-ended questions stimulate discussion and exploration, helping children develop the skills needed to tackle complex problems and make informed decisions.

The power of questions extends to the development of communication skills. Asking and answering questions are fundamental aspects of effective communication. When children ask questions, they practice articulating their thoughts and expressing their curiosity. This process helps them develop their verbal and non-verbal communication skills. Similarly, answering questions requires children to listen actively, process information, and respond thoughtfully. These interactions help children build their vocabulary, improve their language skills, and enhance their ability to engage in meaningful conversations. Encouraging children to ask questions in social settings, such as during group activities or family discussions, helps them develop the confidence to participate in and contribute to conversations.

Socially, questions play a crucial role in building relationships and fostering empathy. When children ask questions about others' experiences, feelings, and perspectives, they develop a deeper understanding of and connection with those around them. This practice of asking empathetic questions helps children learn to appreciate diversity and respect different viewpoints. For example, asking a classmate about their favorite book or a new student about their previous school can help build rapport and establish friendships. Encouraging children to ask questions that show interest in others' lives fosters a sense of community and belonging.

Emotionally, questions can be powerful tools for self-reflection and emotional regulation. Encouraging children to ask questions about their own feelings and experiences helps them develop self-awareness and emotional intelligence. Questions like "Why am I feeling upset?" or "What can I do to feel better?" guide children in exploring their emotions and finding constructive ways to manage them. This practice of self-inquiry helps children develop coping strategies and resilience, enabling them to navigate challenges and setbacks more effectively. Additionally, when adults model asking reflective questions about their own emotions and experiences, they demonstrate healthy emotional regulation and self-care practices for children to emulate.

In educational settings, the power of questions is evident in the practice of inquiry-based learning. This approach to education emphasizes the importance of students' questions in guiding the learning process. Inquiry-based learning encourages students to take an active role in their education by asking questions, conducting research, and presenting their findings. This student-centered approach fosters a sense of ownership and responsibility for learning, making education more engaging and meaningful. By encouraging students to ask questions and explore topics of interest, educators can create a dynamic and interactive learning environment that promotes critical thinking, creativity, and problem-solving.

Questions also play a crucial role in fostering creativity and innovation. When children are encouraged to ask "What if?" and "Why not?" they begin to think beyond the status quo and explore new possibilities. These types of questions stimulate imaginative thinking and encourage children to challenge assumptions and explore alternative solutions. For example, asking "What if we could build a robot that helps with household chores?" can inspire children to explore robotics, engineering, and programming. Encouraging children to ask creative questions helps them develop the skills and mindset needed for innovation and entrepreneurship.

Parents and educators can support the development of questioning skills by creating an environment that values and encourages curiosity. Providing opportunities for exploration and discovery, such as hands-on activities, field trips, and experiments, helps stimulate children's natural curiosity and desire to learn. Additionally, modeling inquisitive behavior by asking questions and seeking answers together with children demonstrates the importance of lifelong learning and intellectual curiosity.

One effective way to encourage questioning is through storytelling and literature. Reading books that feature curious and inquisitive characters can inspire children to ask their own questions and explore new ideas. Discussing stories and asking questions about the characters, plot, and themes can deepen children's understanding and encourage them to think critically about what they read. For example, asking questions like "Why do you think the character made that choice?" or "What do you think will happen next?" stimulates discussion and analysis, helping children develop their comprehension and critical thinking skills.

Encouraging children to keep a question journal can also be a valuable practice. A question journal provides a space for children to write down their questions, thoughts, and observations. This practice helps children develop the habit of inquiry and reflection. Reviewing the journal together with a parent or educator can provide opportunities for discussion, research, and exploration. This practice not only encourages curiosity but also helps children develop their writing and organizational skills.

Another effective strategy is to create a question-friendly classroom or home environment. Displaying question prompts, such as "What do you wonder about?" or "How can we find out?" can inspire children to think critically and ask questions. Providing resources, such as books, websites, and tools, that support inquiry and exploration helps children find answers to their questions and deepen their understanding. Encouraging collaborative questioning, where children work together to explore a topic or solve a problem, fosters a sense of teamwork and shared learning.

Recognizing and celebrating the power of questions is crucial for reinforcing their importance. Acknowledging and praising children's curiosity, effort, and insights encourages them to continue asking questions and seeking knowledge. Creating opportunities for children to share their questions and discoveries, such as through presentations, projects, or discussions, provides a platform for them to express their curiosity and creativity. Celebrating questioning and inquiry helps build a culture of learning and intellectual exploration.

The power of questions in childhood development is profound and far-reaching. Questions stimulate curiosity, drive learning, and foster critical thinking, communication, and social-emotional skills.

Encouraging a questioning mindset helps children become active and engaged learners, capable of independent thought and problem-solving. By creating an environment that values and supports inquiry, parents and educators can nurture children's natural curiosity and help them develop the skills and mindset needed for lifelong learning and success. Through the practice of asking and answering questions, children gain a deeper understanding of the world, build meaningful relationships, and develop the intellectual and emotional tools needed to navigate the complexities of life.

ᗞᗞᗞ

"Collaboration and teamwork teach children the value of different perspectives and collective effort. Working together on creative projects builds strong, supportive relationships. These experiences foster a sense of community and shared achievement."

❦❦❦

NINETEEN

CREATIVE CHALLENGES AND COMPETITIONS

Creative challenges and competitions play a significant role in nurturing a child's development, offering opportunities to enhance their cognitive abilities, build self-esteem, and foster a spirit of healthy competition. Engaging in these activities helps children develop critical thinking skills, encourages innovation, and provides a platform to showcase their talents. These experiences are valuable not only for personal growth but also for preparing children for future academic and professional success.

One of the primary benefits of creative challenges and competitions is the stimulation of cognitive development. When children participate in these activities, they are required to think outside the box, solve problems creatively, and come up with innovative solutions. These processes engage different parts of the brain, promoting cognitive flexibility and enhancing problem-solving abilities. For example, participating in a science fair might require children to design experiments, formulate hypotheses, and analyze data, which strengthens their analytical and critical thinking skills.

Similarly, a writing competition encourages children to develop their language skills, structure their thoughts, and express their ideas clearly and creatively.

Creative challenges also provide a platform for children to explore and develop their talents. Whether it's art, music, writing, or science, these competitions allow children to delve deeply into their areas of interest and showcase their abilities. This focused exploration helps children develop specialized skills and gain confidence in their talents. For instance, an art competition might motivate a young artist to refine their techniques and experiment with new styles, while a robotics competition could inspire a budding engineer to learn coding and mechanical design. These experiences not only enhance specific skills but also contribute to a child's overall sense of competence and self-worth.

Building self-esteem is another significant advantage of participating in creative challenges and competitions. Successfully completing a challenge or winning a competition provides a sense of accomplishment and boosts a child's confidence. Even when children do not win, the process of participating, striving to do their best, and receiving constructive feedback can be incredibly empowering. It teaches them that effort and perseverance are valuable, regardless of the outcome. This mindset helps children develop resilience and a positive attitude towards challenges, which are crucial traits for personal and academic success.

Creative competitions also encourage a spirit of healthy competition. Competing with peers in a supportive and structured environment teaches children the importance of striving for excellence while maintaining respect and sportsmanship. They learn to appreciate others' talents and efforts, which fosters empathy and collaboration. For example, in a debate competition, children must not only present their arguments effectively but also listen to and respect opposing viewpoints. This experience helps them understand the value of different perspectives and the importance of constructive dialogue. Learning to compete fairly and graciously is an essential life skill that prepares children for the competitive nature of the real world.

These challenges and competitions also provide valuable opportunities for feedback and improvement. Constructive feedback from judges, mentors, and peers helps children understand their strengths and areas for growth. This feedback is crucial for personal development, as it guides children in refining their skills and improving their performance. For example, a writing competition might include detailed feedback on narrative structure, grammar, and creativity, which can help a young writer enhance their craft. Learning to accept and utilize feedback positively also teaches children the importance of continuous improvement and lifelong learning.

The collaborative aspect of many creative challenges and competitions further enriches the learning experience. Working in teams, whether it's for a group project, a drama competition, or a sports event, teaches children valuable interpersonal skills. They learn to communicate effectively, delegate tasks, and support each other's efforts. These experiences foster teamwork and cooperation, essential skills for success in both personal and professional contexts. For instance, participating in a team-based science competition requires children to collaborate on research, share ideas, and combine their efforts to achieve a common goal. This collaborative process helps them develop a sense of camaraderie and collective achievement.

Moreover, creative challenges and competitions expose children to real-world applications of their skills and knowledge. They learn to apply theoretical concepts in practical scenarios, which deepens their understanding and makes learning more relevant and engaging. For example, a math competition might involve solving complex problems or developing algorithms, which demonstrates the practical utility of mathematical concepts. Similarly, a business competition might require children to develop a marketing plan or launch a startup idea, providing them with insights into the entrepreneurial world. These real-world applications not only enhance learning but also inspire children to pursue their interests and passions in future careers.

Participation in creative challenges and competitions also helps children develop time management and organizational skills. Preparing for a competition often requires significant planning, practice, and dedication. Children learn to set goals, prioritize tasks, and manage their time effectively to meet deadlines. These skills are transferable to other areas of life, including academic work and personal projects. For instance, preparing for a music competition might involve setting a practice schedule, learning new pieces, and refining performance techniques, all of which require careful time management and discipline. Developing these skills early on prepares children for the demands of higher education and professional life.

Encouraging children to take part in a variety of challenges and competitions can broaden their horizons and expose them to new interests and opportunities. Trying different activities helps children discover their strengths and preferences, and it can open up new pathways for exploration and growth. For example, a child who participates in a poetry competition might discover a passion for writing, while another who competes in a coding challenge might find an interest in computer science. These diverse experiences enrich a child's development and contribute to a well-rounded skill set.

Parents and educators play a crucial role in supporting children's participation in creative challenges and competitions. Providing encouragement, resources, and guidance helps children navigate these experiences positively. It's important to create a supportive environment where children feel motivated to take on challenges and are not discouraged by the fear of failure. Encouraging a growth mindset, where effort and learning are valued over winning, helps children develop resilience and a positive attitude towards competition. For example, praising a child's effort and improvement, regardless of the competition outcome, reinforces the importance of persistence and learning.

Additionally, parents and educators can help children select competitions that align with their interests and strengths. Identifying activities that match a child's passions ensures that the experience is enjoyable and meaningful. It's also important to ensure that the level of competition is appropriate for the child's age and skill level, as this helps build confidence and provides a positive experience. For instance, a young artist might benefit from participating in local art contests before progressing to national or international competitions. This gradual progression helps children build their skills and confidence over time.

Providing opportunities for reflection and learning after competitions is also essential. Encouraging children to reflect on their experiences, identify what they learned, and consider how they can improve in the future fosters a mindset of continuous growth and development. This reflection can involve discussions, journaling, or creating a portfolio of their work. For example, after a debate competition, children might reflect on their preparation, performance, and feedback, and set goals for future improvement. This reflective practice helps children internalize their learning and apply it to future challenges.

Finally, celebrating children's achievements and efforts is crucial for reinforcing the value of creative challenges and competitions. Recognizing and celebrating their hard work, creativity, and accomplishments boosts their self-esteem and motivates them to continue pursuing their interests. Celebrations can take many forms, such as awards ceremonies, showcases, or family gatherings, and they provide an opportunity to acknowledge the child's dedication and success. For example, hosting an art exhibit to display a child's artwork or organizing a recital to showcase their musical talents creates a sense of pride and accomplishment.

Creative challenges and competitions offer numerous benefits for children's development, including cognitive growth, skill development, self-esteem, and social interaction. These activities encourage critical thinking, innovation, and a spirit of healthy competition, preparing children for future academic and professional success. By providing opportunities for exploration, offering support and encouragement, fostering a growth mindset, and celebrating achievements, parents and educators can help children thrive in these experiences. Through participation in creative challenges and competitions, children develop the skills, confidence, and resilience needed to pursue their passions and achieve their full potential.

ᐅᐅᐅ

"Providing opportunities for exploration and discovery helps children find their passions. It allows them to pursue their interests with enthusiasm. This journey of self-discovery is essential for personal growth."

ᗡᗡᗡ

TWENTY

CELEBRATING CREATIVE ACHIEVEMENTS

Celebrating creative achievements in children is a fundamental aspect of fostering their growth and development. Recognizing and honoring their creative endeavors not only boosts their self-esteem but also encourages further exploration and engagement in creative activities. Celebrations provide a platform for children to showcase their talents, receive positive feedback, and feel valued for their efforts. These acknowledgments are crucial for nurturing a child's passion and perseverance, instilling a sense of accomplishment, and promoting a lifelong love for creativity.

One of the key benefits of celebrating creative achievements is the positive impact on a child's self-esteem and confidence. When children see that their creative efforts are recognized and appreciated, they feel a sense of pride and validation. This recognition reinforces their belief in their abilities and motivates them to continue pursuing their interests. For instance, displaying a child's artwork prominently at home or in a public space, such as a school gallery, sends a powerful message that their work is valued. This visible acknowledgment can inspire children to take more creative risks and express themselves more freely.

Encouraging creativity through celebration also fosters intrinsic motivation. Children who experience the joy of having their creative efforts celebrated are more likely to engage in creative activities for the sheer pleasure and satisfaction they bring, rather than for external rewards. This intrinsic motivation is crucial for sustained engagement and deep learning. For example, a child who loves to write stories might be motivated to write more if their work is celebrated through a family reading night or publication in a school magazine. This intrinsic motivation helps children develop a genuine love for creative pursuits, which can lead to lifelong hobbies and even careers in creative fields.

Celebrating creative achievements also promotes a growth mindset, where children understand that effort and perseverance lead to improvement and success. By focusing on the process of creation rather than just the final product, celebrations can highlight the importance of hard work and dedication. This approach helps children appreciate that creativity involves trial and error, experimentation, and learning from mistakes. For instance, a child who is learning to play a musical instrument might be celebrated not just for a flawless performance but also for their consistent practice and progress over time. This emphasis on growth and effort encourages children to embrace challenges and persist in the face of setbacks.

Moreover, celebrating creative achievements helps to reinforce the value of creativity itself. In a world that often prioritizes standardized testing and academic achievement, it is important to show children that creativity is also highly valued and worthy of recognition. This validation can encourage children to explore their creative potential and see it as an important part of their identity. For example, schools that hold annual talent shows, art fairs, or creative writing contests send a clear message that creative endeavors are as important as academic achievements. This balance helps children develop a well-rounded sense of self and recognize the diverse ways they can contribute to the world.

Celebrations also provide opportunities for social connection and community building. When children's creative achievements are celebrated in communal settings, such as family gatherings, school events, or community festivals, it fosters a sense of belonging and collective pride. These events allow children to share their work with others, receive positive feedback, and see the impact of their creativity on their community. For instance, a community theater production involving children can bring together families, friends, and neighbors, creating a supportive environment where children's talents are celebrated and appreciated. These communal celebrations strengthen social bonds and create lasting memories.

Encouraging reflection and self-assessment is another important aspect of celebrating creative achievements. By involving children in the celebration process, such as asking them to present their work, explain their creative process, or share what they learned, children develop a deeper understanding of their own growth and achievements. This reflection helps them recognize their strengths and identify areas for further development. For example, after a school science fair, children might be asked to discuss their projects, what challenges they faced, and how they overcame them. This reflective practice enhances self-awareness and fosters a continuous improvement mindset.

Parents and educators play a crucial role in creating opportunities to celebrate creative achievements. Simple yet meaningful gestures, such as giving verbal praise, writing encouraging notes, or creating dedicated spaces for displaying children's work, can have a profound impact. For instance, a "wall of fame" at home or in the classroom where children's creative works are showcased can serve as a constant reminder of their accomplishments and potential. Additionally, organizing special events, such as award ceremonies, exhibitions, or performances, provides formal recognition and celebrates children's creativity on a larger scale.

Technology can also be leveraged to celebrate creative achievements. Digital platforms, such as social media, blogs, and online portfolios, offer new and exciting ways to showcase children's work to a broader audience. Sharing children's creative projects online allows them to receive feedback from a diverse group of people, including peers, teachers, and family members from different locations. For example, a child who creates digital art can share their work on a social media platform, receiving likes, comments, and shares from a global audience. This online recognition can boost their confidence and provide motivation to continue developing their skills.

Furthermore, celebrating creative achievements helps children see the real-world applications and relevance of their creativity. When their work is recognized and celebrated, children understand that their creative efforts can have a meaningful impact beyond personal satisfaction. For instance, a child who writes a compelling story or designs an innovative project might be celebrated through publication in a local newspaper or recognition in a community awards program. This recognition helps children see the broader significance of their creativity and inspires them to use their talents to make a positive difference in the world.

Recognizing and celebrating creative achievements also promotes equity and inclusivity. By valuing diverse forms of creativity, we acknowledge that every child has unique talents and contributions to offer. Celebrations that highlight a wide range of creative expressions, from visual arts and music to dance, drama, and creative writing, ensure that all children feel valued and included. For example, a school that celebrates creativity through various clubs and events, such as art exhibits, music concerts, drama performances, and literary magazines, provides multiple platforms for children to showcase their talents. This inclusive approach helps children from diverse backgrounds feel recognized and appreciated for their unique contributions.

Encouraging peer recognition and support is another valuable aspect of celebrating creative achievements. When children celebrate each other's successes, it fosters a positive and supportive environment where everyone feels motivated and inspired. Peer recognition can be encouraged through collaborative projects, group exhibitions, and peer feedback sessions. For example, a classroom where students regularly share their creative work and provide positive feedback to each other cultivates a culture of mutual respect and encouragement. This peer support helps children feel more confident in their abilities and more motivated to pursue their creative interests.

Finally, celebrating creative achievements lays the foundation for lifelong creativity and innovation. When children experience the joy and satisfaction of being recognized for their creative efforts, they are more likely to continue engaging in creative activities throughout their lives. This sustained engagement in creativity can lead to personal fulfillment, professional success, and the ability to contribute to society in meaningful ways. For instance, children who are encouraged and celebrated for their creativity may grow up to become artists, writers, inventors, or entrepreneurs who use their talents to drive innovation and positive change.

Celebrating creative achievements in children is essential for fostering their growth, development, and well-being. Recognizing and honoring their creative efforts boosts self-esteem, encourages intrinsic motivation, promotes a growth mindset, and reinforces the value of creativity. Celebrations provide opportunities for social connection, community building, reflection, and self-assessment.

Parents, educators, and communities play a crucial role in creating opportunities to celebrate children's creative achievements, leveraging technology, and promoting equity and inclusivity.

By celebrating creativity, we inspire children to continue exploring their passions, develop their talents, and contribute to the world in meaningful ways. Through this recognition and celebration, we nurture a generation of confident, innovative, and fulfilled individuals who see creativity as a vital and valued part of their lives.

❦❦❦

"A supportive and nurturing environment is crucial for fostering creativity. It gives children the freedom to explore and the confidence to express themselves. In such an environment, their potential knows no bounds."

❧❧❧

TWENTY-ONE
SUMMARY

Throughout childhood, a myriad of activities and influences shape a child's development, fostering cognitive, emotional, social, and physical growth. By exploring various facets of creative and intellectual pursuits, children gain essential skills and build a foundation for lifelong learning and success. This comprehensive journey through childhood development highlights the importance of encouraging creativity, celebrating achievements, and supporting individual interests while maintaining a balanced approach to structure and freedom.

One crucial aspect of nurturing children's development is the role of creativity in various activities, from cooking and baking to engaging in role-playing and drama. These activities stimulate cognitive growth, enhance problem-solving abilities, and promote emotional well-being. For instance, creative cooking and baking provide children with opportunities to develop fine motor skills, practice math and science concepts, and explore different cultures through culinary traditions. Similarly, role-playing and drama allow children to express their emotions, build empathy, and develop communication skills by stepping into different roles and scenarios.

In addition to creative pursuits, the power of questions plays a significant role in children's cognitive and emotional development. Encouraging children to ask questions fosters curiosity, drives learning, and helps them develop critical thinking skills. By creating an environment that values and supports inquiry, parents and educators can nurture children's natural curiosity and help them become active, engaged learners. This approach not only enhances their understanding of the world but also builds their confidence and resilience.

Balancing structure and freedom is another essential aspect of supporting children's growth. Providing a stable environment with routines and clear expectations helps children feel secure and understand boundaries. At the same time, allowing them the freedom to explore their interests and make choices fosters independence, creativity, and personal growth. This balance is crucial for helping children develop self-discipline, time management skills, and a sense of responsibility while also encouraging them to take risks and learn from their experiences.

Supporting individual interests is vital for nurturing children's passions and fostering a love for learning. By recognizing and valuing each child's unique preferences, providing resources and opportunities for exploration, and offering encouragement and positive reinforcement, parents and educators can help children develop their talents and build self-confidence. This approach not only enhances their skills in specific areas but also promotes a sense of purpose and intrinsic motivation, which are essential for lifelong learning and personal fulfillment.

Creative challenges and competitions offer valuable opportunities for children to showcase their talents, receive feedback, and build resilience. Participating in these activities helps children develop critical thinking skills, encourages innovation, and fosters a spirit of healthy competition. These experiences also provide opportunities for collaboration, social interaction, and real-world applications of their skills and knowledge. By supporting children's participation in creative challenges and competitions, parents and educators can help them build confidence, develop a growth mindset, and prepare for future academic and professional success.

Exploring different cultures is another important aspect of childhood development, promoting cultural awareness, empathy, and open-mindedness. Exposure to diverse traditions, languages, cuisines, and histories helps children develop a broader perspective and a deeper appreciation for cultural diversity. This exploration fosters a sense of curiosity and respect for different perspectives, enhancing their social and emotional skills. By creating opportunities for children to learn about and engage with various cultures, parents and educators can help them become informed and compassionate global citizens.

Nature and outdoor exploration also play a significant role in children's development, offering numerous physical, cognitive, emotional, and social benefits. Spending time outdoors and engaging with nature allows children to explore the natural world, develop physical skills, and build resilience. These activities promote a sense of wonder and curiosity, fostering a love for learning and environmental stewardship. Encouraging children to spend time in nature and providing opportunities for outdoor exploration helps them develop a strong connection to the environment and a sense of responsibility for its preservation.

Storytelling and creative writing are powerful tools for enhancing children's language skills, stimulating imagination, and fostering emotional growth. Engaging in these activities helps children develop a rich vocabulary, understand sentence structure and grammar, and express their thoughts and emotions. Storytelling and creative writing also promote cognitive development by encouraging critical thinking and problem-solving skills. By providing opportunities for children to create and share their stories, parents and educators can help them develop a love for literature and communication, enhancing their overall development.

Music and movement activities are essential for children's physical, cognitive, emotional, and social growth. These activities help children develop motor skills, coordination, and balance while also stimulating brain development and enhancing language skills. Music and movement provide valuable opportunities for self-expression and emotional regulation, promoting a sense of well-being and happiness. Additionally, these activities encourage social interaction and collaboration, helping children develop important social skills such as empathy, cooperation, and respect for others.

Art and craft activities offer numerous benefits for children's development, fostering creativity, fine motor skills, and emotional expression. Engaging in these activities allows children to explore their imagination, develop their artistic skills, and express their emotions in a safe and supportive environment. Art and craft activities also promote cognitive development by encouraging problem-solving, critical thinking, and spatial awareness. By providing a variety of materials and opportunities for creative exploration, parents and educators can help children develop a love for art and creativity, enhancing their overall development.

Imaginative play and role-playing are crucial for children's social and emotional development, providing opportunities for them to explore different perspectives, build empathy, and develop communication skills. Engaging in imaginative play helps children understand and manage their emotions, fostering emotional intelligence and resilience. These activities also encourage social interaction and cooperation, helping children develop important interpersonal skills. By creating opportunities for imaginative play and providing a supportive environment, parents and educators can help children develop a strong sense of self and build healthy relationships.

Building and construction play is essential for children's physical, cognitive, and social development, offering opportunities for them to explore their creativity, solve problems, and develop fine and gross motor skills. Engaging in these activities helps children develop their spatial awareness, understanding of cause and effect, and ability to think critically and analytically. Building and construction play also promotes collaboration and teamwork, helping children develop important social skills such as communication, cooperation, and conflict resolution. By providing a variety of materials and opportunities for building and construction play, parents and educators can help children develop a love for exploration and creativity.

Supporting a growth mindset is crucial for children's development, helping them understand that abilities and intelligence can be developed through effort, perseverance, and learning. Encouraging a growth mindset involves teaching children about the principles of growth, using growth-oriented language and praise, modeling positive attitudes, and providing a supportive environment for exploration and learning. This approach helps children develop resilience, a positive attitude towards challenges, and a love for learning, enhancing their overall development and well-being.

Technology and digital creativity play a significant role in contemporary childhood development, offering numerous benefits for cognitive, emotional, social, and technical growth. Providing access to creative tools, encouraging collaborative projects, and integrating digital creativity into education helps children harness the full potential of the digital world. By balancing screen time with hands-on, real-world experiences, staying informed about technological advancements, and celebrating children's digital creations, parents and educators can support their growth and development in a dynamic and enriching way.

Collaboration and teamwork are essential skills for children's development, helping them navigate social dynamics, build strong relationships, and achieve common goals. Engaging in collaborative activities teaches children the importance of communication, cooperation, and empathy. These experiences foster a sense of belonging and community, enhancing their social and emotional skills. By creating opportunities for meaningful collaboration, providing guidance and feedback, and modeling effective teamwork, parents and educators can help children develop these critical skills and thrive in various aspects of life.

In summary, childhood development is a multifaceted journey that involves nurturing creativity, encouraging exploration, supporting individual interests, and maintaining a balance between structure and freedom. By recognizing and celebrating children's creative achievements, providing opportunities for exploration and discovery, and fostering a supportive and inclusive environment, parents and educators can help children develop the skills, confidence, and resilience needed to navigate the complexities of life and achieve their full potential. Through this holistic approach, children are empowered to pursue their passions, develop their talents, and contribute to the world in meaningful ways.

❧❧❧

Citation And References

This book represents the culmination of extensive research and meticulous analysis, incorporating a diverse range of sources, including numerous books, scholarly studies, and personal experiences. Additionally, I have scoured various websites to gather relevant information and data essential for the compilation of this work. I have taken every precaution to ensure the accuracy of the information presented and have diligently cited all sources to acknowledge their contributions.

Despite these efforts, the possibility of inadvertent errors remains. I deeply value the insights of my readers and appreciate any feedback that can help identify and rectify such inaccuracies. I encourage you to bring any discrepancies to my attention.

Your feedback is not only welcome but crucial, as it will aid in correcting current editions and enhancing the content of future ones. I am committed to maintaining the highest standards of accuracy and reliability in my work and thank you for your support and understanding.

Additionally, I firmly uphold the principle of freedom of speech and expression as guaranteed under Article 19(1)(a) of the Constitution of India, and I respect the diverse viewpoints and expressions of all readers.

ღღღ

Other Books Of The Author

1. Empowering Minds: A Journey into Women's Self-Discovery and Power
2. The Dynamics of Motivation: Catalyzing Thought into Action
3. Meditation and Mental Well Being: The Path to Inner Peace and Clarity
4. The Psychology of Child Education: Nurturing Future Generations
5. Ethical Enlightenment: A Modern Guide to Living with Integrity
6. Voices of Empowerment: Stories of Women Rising Against Odds
7. Social Psychology in Everyday Life: Understanding Human Connections
8. The Essence of Motivational Speaking: Inspiring Change in Others
9. Balancing Acts: Women, Work, and the Will to Lead
10. Guiding with Grace: Raising Children with Compassion and Awareness
11. The Power of Positive Aging: Embracing Life After Fifty
12. Building Resilient Communities: Social Work in Action
13. The Ethical Educator: Principles for Teaching and Learning
14. From Insight to Impact: Social Psychology for a Better World
15. The Ethics of Empathy: A Guide to Ethical Living
16. The Science of Empowering the Self: Navigating Life's Challenges with Psychological Wisdom
17. The Mindful Conscious Leader: Meditation Techniques for Modern Management
18. Pioneering Spirit: Women's Pathways to Leadership and Empowerment
19. Feeling to Healing: The Role of Emotional Intelligence in Child Development
20. Transformative Talks and Words of Inspiration: Insights into Motivational Oratory

21. Green Ethics: A Path to Sustainable Living
22. Spiritual Integrity: Navigating Life with Moral Compassion
23. Clean Living, Clean Society: The Ethics of Cleanliness
24. Patriotic Spirits: Building a Nation on Positive Attitudes
25. Innovative Integrity & Vibrant Visions: The Ethical and Entrepreneurial Spirit of Gujarat
26. Youthful Visions, Endless Possibilities: Inspiring Ethics and Motivation in Children
27. Living Your Legacy: How to Motivate Others by Living Your Values
28. Secret of Healing Conversations: Ethical Practices in Counselling and Therapy
29. Creative Kindness: Crafting a Life of Compassion and Creativity
30. The Power of Appreciation: How Gratitude Can Transform Your Relationships
31. Bhagavad-Gita: Messages
32. Science of Art: The New Frontier of Fashion Modernism
33. Vivekananda's Virtues: A Blueprint for Modern Living
34. Empower Her: Navigating the Path to Women's Entrepreneurship
35. The Boundless Classroom: Innovations in Global Education
36. The Language of Leadership: Communicating with Authenticity and Impact
37. The Warrior's Mantra: Deciphering the Hanuman Chalisa
38. Echoes of Empathy: Transformative Stories of Social Service
39. Artful Living: Cultivating Creativity in Your Daily Routine
40. Finding Your Why: Discovering Your Passions and Charting Your Course
41. The Role of Social Media in Shaping Self-Esteem and Interpersonal Relationships among Adolescents
42. Karma's Tapestry: Weaving a Life of Selfless Service
43. Altruistic Alchemy: Transforming Lives Through Giving
44. The Blueprint of Pro-Activeness and Productivity: Crafting Habits for Success
45. The Simplicity with Grounded Wisdom: Embracing Authenticity

in a Complex World

46. Secret of Solopreneur's Odyssey: Navigating the Path to Self-Employment
47. Exploring Tapestry of Peace: Global Perspectives on Harmony
48. The Art and Actions of Connection: Mastering Communication for Impact
49. She Governs and at the Helm: Strategies for Political Empowerment
50. Rising Above and Rising with Grace: A Woman's Roadmap to Career Mastery
51. The Effect of Networking & Connectedness: Building Strategic Alliances for Women
52. Beyond his Barriers: Women Thriving in Male-Dominated Fields
53. Secret of Inner Compass: Navigating Life with Intuition
54. Creative & Pro-Active Muses: A Celebration of Women in the Arts
55. Unburdened: The Art of Releasing the Past
56. Amplified Voices: Speeches of Women that Astonished the World
57. Secret of Manifesting Dreams: A Woman's Guide to Intentional Living
58. Ethics and Value Based Education: Reimagining Japan's School System
59. The Moral Compass Curriculum: A Holistic Approach
60. Tech with Heart: Integrating Ethics into Digital Learning
61. Honoring Virtue: Recognizing Ethical Excellence in Education
62. Raising Good Humans: A Guide to Character Development
63. The Spark Within: Nurturing Creativity in Children
64. The Teenager Whisperer: Navigating Adolescence with Grace
65. Igniting a Passion for Learning: Inspiring Lifelong Curiosity
66. The Habit Lab: Cultivating Positive Behaviors in Children
67. Seeds of Empathy: Fostering Compassion in Young Hearts
68. The Reading Revolution: Inspiring a Love of Books in Children
69. The Learning Brain: Unlocking the Secrets of Student Success
70. Teaching for All: Differentiated Instruction Strategies
71. The Time Alchemist: Mastering Time Management for Peak Performance

72. The Resilience Factor: Transforming Setbacks into Stepping Stones
73. The Healing Touch of Nature: An Introduction to Naturopathy
74. Echoes of the Past: Healing Through Past Life Regression
75. The Spiritual Healer's Handbook: Exploring Energy Medicine
76. Crystal Clarity: Unveiling the Power of Gemstones
77. The Dream Weaver's Guide: Decoding the Language of Dreams
78. Emotional Alchemy: Transforming Pain into Power
79. Sonic Serenity: Harnessing Sound for Stress Relief
80. The Entrepreneur's Playbook: Launching Your Business with Confidence
81. Productivity Unleashed: Time Management Strategies for Entrepreneurs
82. The Problem Solver's Toolkit: Creative Solutions for Business Challenges
83. The Future is Now: Emerging Trends in Business
84. The Curious Explorer: A Child's Guide to Scientific Discovery
85. Digital Pioneers: Empowering Kids in the Tech World
86. The Young Philosopher's Guide: Exploring Life's Big Questions
87. Finding Your Voice: Communication Skills for Confident Kids
88. Nature's Playground: A Child's Guide to Outdoor Adventure
89. Growing a Greener Tomorrow: A Guide to Tree Planting & Conservation
90. Driving with Purpose: Ethical Choices on the Road
91. The Healing Touch: Cultivating Compassion in Healthcare
92. Navigating the Digital Landscape: Ethics in the Age of Social Media
93. The Ethical Closet: A Guide to Sustainable Fashion
94. The Mindful Voyager: Sustainable Travel Practices
95. The Feminine Divine: Honoring the Goddesses of India
96. Sacred Sounds: Chanting Your Way to Inner Peace
97. The Yoga Path: Uniting with the Divine Within
98. Rites of Passage: Creating Meaningful Ceremonies
99. The Chakra System: A Map of Inner Transformation
100. Spiritual Sangha: Finding Community through Satsang and

Bhajan

101. Pilgrimage of the Soul: Spiritual Journeys in India

❦❦❦

Contact

Dr. Minakshi Bansal
Social Activist
Ahmedabad, Gujarat, Bharat
minakshiindiag20@yahoo.com

ᐅᐅᐅ

|| LOKAHA SAMASTHAHA SUKHINO BHAVANTU ||